SpringerBriefs in Linguistics

A platform for peer-reviewed short research monographs on all topics in the study of language, including syntax, semantics, philosophy of language, sociolinguistics, psycholinguistics, cognitive linguistics, translation studies, languages and literature, computational linguistics, as well as cross- and interdisciplinary studies in linguistics, and across all schools of thought and all methodologies. Volumes offer concise summaries of cutting-edge research and practical applications across a wide spectrum of fields within linguistics. Compact volumes of 50 to 125 pages cover a range of content from theoretical to experimental and applied research in linguistics. Typical topics might include: • A timely report of state-of-the art analytical techniques • A bridge between new research results published in journal articles and a contextual literature review • A snapshot of a hot or emerging topic • An in-depth case study or fieldwork results • A presentation of core concepts that students must understand in order to make independent contributions The publishing editor, Christopher Coughlin, welcomes your proposals and ideas for monographs that fit in this series.

More information about this series at https://link.springer.com/bookseries/11940

Helen Goodluck

Complex Syntax in the Language of Persons with Down Syndrome

Springer

Helen Goodluck
Department of Language Science
and Linguistics
University of York
York, UK

ISSN 2197-0009 ISSN 2197-0017 (electronic)
SpringerBriefs in Linguistics
ISBN 978-3-030-96439-9 ISBN 978-3-030-96440-5 (eBook)
https://doi.org/10.1007/978-3-030-96440-5

This Springer imprint is published by the registered company Springer Nature Switzerland AG
The registered company address is: Gewerbestrasse 11, 6330 Cham, Switzerland

In memory of

Alice Eriks-Brophy

1955–2019

Preface

This research began as a collaborative effort between myself and Alice Eriks-Brophy, both then at the University of Ottawa (in the Linguistics Department and the Department of Speech-Language Pathology respectively). Subsequently I moved to the University of York in England and Alice moved to the University of Toronto, where Alice collected the majority of the data between 2000 and 2008.

Particular thanks go to Danijela Stojanović, who worked on the project in 2000–2001; she was largely responsible for the materials in the experiments reported in Chap. 5. Thanks also to Jen Nixon for administrative help. The data was collected with the help of Danijela, Toni Blanchard and Chantale Mayer (University of Ottawa), volunteers from the Carleton University Cognitive Science Program and Nadia Abisaleh and Laurie Graham (University of Toronto). Thanks to Professor Leonard Abbeduto (University of California Davis), who provided input on the introductory and concluding chapters and to an anonymous reviewer for comments on the whole manuscript.

I have used that pronoun "we" in writing this report. This seems wholly appropriate because the research was very much a collaborative effort. However, neither Alice nor Danijela should bear any responsibility for errors or misrepresentations in the manuscript—those are mine alone! This project has taken many years before publication, and we constantly played catch-up with the literature. Although we may not always have been successful in taking account of recent results, we hope that the data we present may contribute to understanding linguistic aspects of Down Syndrome.

Finally, we wholeheartedly thank the persons with Down Syndrome who took part in our study and their carers. The lively company of our participants made the project a pleasure.

York, UK

Helen Goodluck
helen.goodluck@york.ac.uk

Funding Information

This research was funded by a University of Ottawa Interdisciplinary Research Grant in 1998-9 to Alice Eriks-Brophy and Helen Goodluck, a Bloorview Hospital Grant in 1999–2001 to Eriks-Brophy and Goodluck and an Arts and Humanities Research Council of the UK study leave in 2007 to Goodluck.

Ethics Statement

This research was approved by the University of Ottawa Ethics Board for participants tested in Ottawa and by the Ethics Review Unit of the Faculty of Medicine, University of Toronto, for participants tested in Toronto.

Contents

Chapter 1
Introduction

Abstract The chapter begins with a brief review of the literature on the modularity of linguistic, as opposed to other cognitive abilities, in a number of disabled populations. The general characteristics of Down Syndrome (DS) are reviewed, followed by a review of the morphological and syntactic capacity proposed for persons with DS. This is generally regarded as poor, although a small number of cases in which highly developed ability have been reported. An ability to read has been held to enhance language performance in persons with DS; this study aimed to examine the syntactic capacity of persons with DS who were readers.

Keywords Mentally disabled populations · Linguistic ability · Down Syndrome · Reading

1.1 Language Ability in the Absence of Cognitive Skills

Over the past 30 years or more, cases of exceptional linguistic ability in persons with limited intellectual capacities in other areas of cognition have been documented (for breakthrough studies, see Tew 1979; Yamada 1990; Bellugi et al. 1993, 1997; Cromer 1994; Smith and Tsimpli 1995). Different disabilities have been involved: Spina Bifida, Williams Syndrome, or an unclear aetiology. Where administered, the persons scored low on mental age tests, tests that tapped the abilities defined by the psychologist Jean Piaget, visual/spatial tests and tests of an individual's awareness of other people's mental state (Theory of Mind tests). By contrast, some of these persons showed a command of complex syntax and morphology, as evidenced by their ready use of constructions such as embedded complements to verbs, adverbial clauses and relative clauses. This fluency had led to the term 'cocktail party syndrome' (applied to persons with Williams Syndrome and Spina Bifida). This dissociation of linguistic abilities from more general cognitive skills has been interpreted as evidence that the language system is modular, i.e. that language can exist without underpinning from other intellectual skills. Although DS has not been associated with the characteristics of cocktail party syndrome, some cases of exceptional abilities have been documented, as we will see below.

H. Goodluck, *Complex Syntax in the Language of Persons with Down Syndrome*, SpringerBriefs in Linguistics,
https://doi.org/10.1007/978-3-030-96440-5_1

1.2 General Characteristics of DS

DS is the most frequent form of mental retardation, accounting for one in every 700–1000 live births. It is caused by a trisomy of chromosome 21 and is associated generally with mild to moderate retardation, with some individuals falling in the normal IQ range and others being severely retarded (Roizen 2002; Wisniewshi et al. 2006). IQ scores may rapidly decline with age, reflecting a slow developmental rate rather than a loss of previously acquired skills (Carr 1995; Hauser-Cram et al. 2001). Other features associated with DS include hypotonia, congenital heart defects, growth reduction, immune dysfunction and autoimmune disorders, and craniofacial anomalies that contribute to recurrent episodes of otitis media with effusion that may continue throughout the lifespan. Up to 68% of children with DS have hearing losses that may be conductive, sensironeural or mixed (Roizen et al. 1993; Shott et al. 2001). Individuals with DS also show a characteristic profile with respect to aspects of memory, such that implicit or semantic memory abilities appear to be commensurate with overall levels of functioning, while working memory shows a particular weakness in the manipulation of auditory verbal memory, as compared to visual-spatial material; episodic memory is weak in both the verbal and spatial domains (Brock and Jarrold 2005; Devenny 2006). The role of working memory in the language development of persons with DS has produced results that are not entirely consistent. For example, Chapman et al. (2002) found that working memory was a predictor of syntactic production in DS. However, Fortunato-Tavares et al. (2015) found an effect of working memory (as measured by the introduction of an extra Prepositional Phrase in the sentence) had an effect for children with Specific Language Impairment (and typically developing children), but not for participants with Down Syndrome or High Functioning Autism.

Three main aetiological subcategories of DS exist, namely standard trisomy 21, which accounts for 97% of all cases; translocations, accounting for 2% of the total population; and mosaicism, which accounts for the remaining 1% of the population. No major differences in language ability across these subgroups have been reliably demonstrated (Rondal 2006). Chapters in Rondal and Perera (2006) provide reviews of characteristics of the syndrome.

1.3 Language Abilities in Persons with DS

The standard view of the language abilities of persons with DS is that this area of cognitive functioning is one that is particularly impaired, in contrast to the studies of exceptional language abilities sketched for other syndromes in Sect. 1.

A number of studies have compared the abilities of persons with DS to other disabled populations, including Williams Syndrome, Fragile X Syndrome, Specific Language Impairment and Autism (see, for example, Guozzo 2006, Joffe and Varlokosta 2007 and Price et al. 2007 for a comparison with Williams Syndrome and Fragile X Syndrome, and Fortunato-Tavares et al. 2015 for a comparison with Specific Language Impairment and Autism).

The profile of individuals with DS is characterized by relative weaknesses in the domains of receptive and expressive language, reading, writing, and metacognition, while pragmatic abilities are proposed as being an area of relative strength. Individuals with Williams Syndrome present with the exact opposite profile, while persons with Fragile X Syndrome present with a profile of relative weakness in all of these domains. Some researchers, including Chapman (1997, 2006), Fowler (1990) and Miller (1999), argue that vocabulary comprehension in individuals with DS may represent an area of strength, particularly when compared to their syntactic abilities.

With respect to the course of language development, it has been generally agreed that individuals with DS pass through the initial states of language acquisition in a qualitatively similar manner to normally developing children, although at a slower pace. Articulatory development is slower when compared to typically developing peers, and may be accompanied by significantly reduced speech intelligibility (Dodd and Leahy 1989; Roberts et al. 2007; Smith and Oller 1981). Semantic development is typically delayed in proportion to the overall cognitive impairment of the child, yet shows a positive linear relation with mental age (Rondal and Edwards 1997). Multi-word productions may not be observed until age three or four in children with DS. However, the semantic relationships expressed by such utterances are similar to those used by typically developing children (Rondal 2006). Mean Length of Utterance (MLU) values of 1 (one word/morpheme) are reported up to age two, with increases to an MLU of 4 between ages two and nine. Children with typical language development usually have an MLU of 5 or more units by six years of age, while children with DS may not achieve that level until age 11 or 12, and may not progress beyond that level. Increase in MLU in individuals with DS is proposed to be limited by their reduced productive use of articles, prepositions, pronouns, conjunctions, auxiliary verbs and of morphological markers including gender, tense, modality and aspect (O'Neill and Henry 2002; Rondal 2006).

By the time they reach early adolescence, individuals with DS are often described as having reached a plateau in both expressive and receptive language development, stopping at Brown's Linguistic Stage III (Brown 1973), a level typical of three to four year old normally developing children (Fowler 1990; Fowler et al. 1994; Miller 1999; Rondal and Comblain 1996). Evidence from examinations of syntactic comprehension and production in individuals with DS suggests a specific language impairment in the acquisition of morphosyntactic abilities that is linked to mental age (Chapman 1995, 1997; Fowler 1990, Fowler et al. 1994; Hartely 1986; Miller 1988; Joffe and Varlokosta 2007). For example, Fowler et al. (1994) studied the production of language by four children aged 10 to 13 with DS and by one younger subject, who was tested longitudinally between ages 4;3 (years; months) and 7;5. They concluded that the development of their participants stalled at a stage characteristic of typically developing children aged two and a half to three years. Specifically, Fowler et al. found an absence of development of complex syntax; in their words,

> It is difficult to ignore the fact that the stopping point in this group of children [with DS] precedes the dramatic growth in syntactic development that has captured the imagination of linguists. Although this break is implicitly adhered to in child language research (syntacticians study children from age 3 and up; early child language folks study children up to age 3), in the present research it gains some empirical validity as a possible and important difference in language representation (Fowler et al. 1994, p. 135)

In summary, despite the indisputable limitations of language in the majority of persons with DS, the course of language development in this population has generally been considered to be delayed, and ultimately stalled, but not deviant from typical language development. That is, the stages that individuals go through in developing language are similar to those that typically developing children go through, albeit at a slower pace. What is generally absent in individuals with DS, however, is the rapid acquisition of a variety of complex sentence types that is seen in the language of typically developing two to three year olds.[1]

1.4 A More Nuanced Picture

The general picture sketched above—of delayed, and ultimately stalled language development in persons with DS—was the picture prevalent in the literature when we planned the present study in the late 1990s. However, even at that point there were studies that suggested that the prognosis for syntactic development in persons with DS might not be as bleak as Fowler et al. (1994) proposed.

1.4.1 Case Studies

First, there have been reports of highly developed production and comprehension of complex syntax in some individuals with DS. Seagoe (1965, as reported in Rondal 1995, pp. 23–25) documents the case of a young American man with DS who had a sophisticated command of English syntax. The following is an excerpt from his written diary,

> Last night we took the sleeper for Polish frontier. The countryside from Moscow to Polish frontier enroute to Warsaw is like a neglected cemetery. The houses are tumbling down and little agricultural activity. This cold morning it was not uncommon sight to see peasants and their children bare-footed and with overcoats on. Women wait on and cook food in railway depots. The general employment of women in manual work is to let men enter the enormous Russian military services.

(This diary excerpt is from a visit to Europe with his family.) Although there are some errors—the definite article is omitted before 'Polish frontier' and 'wait on' is

[1] More recent research has lowered the age at which infants can recognise syntactic distinctions, using technology that is less demanding of the infant than production of structures (see for example, Seidl et al. 2003).

used intransitively—nonetheless the passage shows a remarkable fluency and a rich vocabulary.

Rondal (1995) reports the case of a French-speaking woman, Françoise, who produced and comprehended highly accurately the syntax of her language. She performed at almost 100% accuracy on the comprehension of active and passive sentences with a variety of verb types (actional ± punctual, and non-actional ± punctual), relative clauses with subject and object gaps, and causative and temporal subordinate clauses. Françoise' conversation shows inter alia appropriate turn taking, appropriate use of definite and indefinite articles and appropriate organization with respect to given-new information. Some failure of text planning is evident, but there are several occasions where she shows sensitivity to her interlocutor's needs—for example, when she provides background information in the following utterance,

> Tandis que moi quand il fait des chaleurs comme ça moi on ne me voit trés rarement à la porte en tous cas
>
> (Whereas me when it is hot like that me one sees me very rarely out of doors anyway).

Françoise' performance on general intelligence measures and memory is generally intermediate between what would be expected of mentally disabled persons and what would be expected of typically developing children/adults.

1.4.2 *Other Studies*

Research published since we began our study argues that knowledge of complex syntax is not necessarily restricted to exceptional 'savant' persons with DS. For example, production data reported by Thordardottir et al. (2002) has also shown the use of a range of complex constructions by persons with DS (this study is examined in more detail in Chap. 4).

1.5 The Importance of Reading

A number of researchers have proposed that early training in reading can contribute to enhanced language performance in persons with DS (Buckley 2007; Buckley and Bird 1993; Buckley et al. 1996; Groen et al. 2006; Hulme et al. 2005; Oelwein 1995). This research supports the view that all children with DS can benefit from being read to and from being taught reading skills. These activities may contribute to gains in speech intelligibility, short term memory, and receptive and productive use of complex syntactic structures. Having recourse to the printed word also reduces the demand on auditory working memory, thought to be an area of particular weakness in individuals with DS (Devenny 2006), freeing valuable resources at the level of working memory that can then be applied to sentence comprehension and production. However, research has also revealed that the contribution of different components of reading ability (comprehension skills and decoding abilities) may be different for persons with DS, even though the overall ability to read is the same as for a non-impaired population (Roch and Levorato 2009).

1.6 Obedience to the Rules of Grammar in the Absence of Morphological Cues

Fowler et al. (1994) and others have noted that the absence or comparative lack of function words (prepositions, articles and other grammatical markers) in the language of children with DS can be taken as evidence of the lack of the morphological underpinning of complex syntax. These two failings (lack of morphological marking and lack of complex syntax) can be viewed as related in the light of linguistic theory (for example, Chomsky 1993), since sentence structure is assumed to involve not only traditional phrase types, such as Verb Phrase and Noun Phrase, but also 'functional' categories. The latter provide an infrastructure over the traditional category types, hosting morphological agreement and sentence embedding. For example, there is a grammatical category and phrase type, Complementizer Phrase (CP), which is lexically filled by, inter alia, the word *that* in English, in sentences such as *John knew that Bud would arrive on time*. The presence of CP in the grammar is essential to the embedding of *Bud would arrive on time* in the example.

However, some research on typical language development argues that the underpinning of complex syntax may be achieved before three years of age, and in the absence of production of the relevant morphology and functional categories (see, for example, Weissenborn et al. 1998). Thus production of such elements may not be a good diagnostic of the presence or absence of syntactic structures with which they are associated. This point is underscored by research by Schaner-Wolles (2000) on persons with DS. Schaner-Wolles reports that in a sentence repetition task, German-speaking persons with DS show evidence of the correct placement of the verb in second position in main clauses; this positioning is standardly analysed as the result of moving the verb from its underlying (sentence final) position. Crucially, the placement of the verb in second position was frequently accomplished without correct marking of the verb as tensed (rather than infinitival), tensing being a prerequisite for verb movement in German. Schaner-Wolles argues that this suggests that persons with DS develop hierarchical syntactic structures independently of knowledge of morphological operations associated with those structures.

1.7 Summary and Goals of the Present Research

We aimed to investigate the extent to which cases such as those reported by Rondal (1995) were cases of 'savant' knowledge, or whether complex syntax was within the reach of persons with DS in more than one or two isolated cases. In what follows we will see that the answer is broadly yes, a finding confirmed by other research published since we began our work (such as the study by Schaner-Wolles cited above).

References

Bellugi, U., P. Wang, and T. Jerrigan. 1993. Dissociation between language and cognitive functions in Williams syndrome. In *Language development in exceptional circumstances*, ed. D. Bishop and K. Mogford. London: Churchill.

Bellugi, U., Z. Lai, and P. Wang. 1997. Language, communication and neural development in Williams syndrome. *Mental Retardation and Developmental Disabilities* 3: 334–342.

Brock, J., and C. Jarrold. 2005. Serial order reconstruction in Down Syndrome: Evidence for a selective deficit in short-term memory. *Journal of Child Psychology and Psychiatry* 46: 304–316.

Brown, R. 1973. *A First Language*. Cambridge, MA: Harvard University Press.

Buckley, S. 2007. Exceptional reading among young people with Down Syndrome. *Down Syndrome Research and Practice* 12: 9–10.

Buckley, S., and G. Bird. 1993. Teaching children with Down Syndrome to read. *Down Syndrome Research and Practice* 1: 34–39.

Buckley S., G. Bird, and A. Byrne. 1996. The practical and theoretical significance of teaching literacy skills to children with Down Syndrome. In *Down Syndrome: Psychological, psychobiological and socioeducational perspectives*, ed. J. Rondal and J. Perera, 119–128. London, UK: Whurr.

Carr, J. 1995. *Down's syndrome: Children growing up*. Cambridge, UK: Cambridge University Press.

Chapman, R. 1995. Language development in children and adolescents with Down Syndrome. In *Handbook of child language*, ed. P. Fletcher and B. MacWhinney, 641–663. Oxford, UK: Blackwell.

Chapman, R. 1997. Language development in children and adolescents with Down Syndrome. *Mental Retardation and Developmental Disabilities Research Reviews* 3: 301–312.

Chapman, R. 2006. Language learning in Down Syndrome: The speech and language profile compared to adolescents with cognitive impairment of unknown origin. *Down Syndrome Research and Practice* 10: 61–66.

Chapman, R., L. Hesketh, and D. Kistler. 2002. Predicting longitudinal change in language production and comprehension in individuals with Down Syndrome: Hierachical linear ordering. *Journal of Speech, Language and Hearing Research* 45: 902–915.

Chomsky, N. 1993. A minimalist program for linguistic theory. In *The view from building 20*, ed. K. Hale and S. J. Keyser. Cambridge, MA: MIT Press.

Cromer, R. 1994. A case study of dissociations between language and cognition. In *Constraints on language acquisition: Studies of atypical children*, ed. H. Tager-Flusberg. Hillsdale, NJ: Lawrence Erlbaum Associates.

Devenny, D. 2006. The contribution of memory to the behavioural phenotype of Down Syndrome. In *Down Syndrome: Neurobehavioral specificity*, ed. J. Rondal and J. Perrera. Hoboken, NJ: Wiley.

Dodd, B., and P. Leahy. 1989. Phonological disorder and mental handicap. In *Language communication in mentally handicapped people*, ed. G. Conti-Ramsden and I. Leuda, 33–56. London: Chapman and Hall.

Fortunato-Tavares, T., S. Andrade, B. Befi-Lopes, S. Limongi, F. Ferdandes, and R. Schwartz. 2015. Syntactic comprehension and working memory in children with specific language impairment or Down Syndrome. *Clinical Linguistics and Phonetics* 29: 499–522.

Fowler, A. 1990. Language abilities in children with Down Syndrome: Evidence for a specific syntactic delay. In *Children with Down Syndrome: A developmental perspective*, ed. D. Cicchette and M. Beeghly. Cambridge, UK: Cambridge University Press.

Fowler, A., R. Gelman and L. Gleitman. 1994. The course of language learning in children with Down Syndrome: Longitudinal and language level comparisons with young normally developing children. In *Constraints on language acquisition: Studies of atypical children*, ed. H. Tager-Flusberg. Hillsdale, NY: Lawrence Erlbaum Associates.

Groen, M., G. Laws, K. Nation, and D. Bishop. 2006. A case of exceptional reading accuracy in a child with Down syndrome: Underlying skills and the relation to reading comprehension. *Cognitive Neuropsychology* 23: 1190–1214.

Guozzo, G. 2006. Learning difficulties in Down Syndrome. In *Down Syndrome: Neurobehavioral specificity*, ed. J. Rondal and J. Perera. Cht. 10. John Wiley and Sons Ltd.

Hartely, X. 1986. A summary of recent research into the development of children with Down Syndrome. *Journal of Mental Deficiency Research* 30: 1–14.

Hauser-Cram, P., M. Warfield, J. Shonkoff, M. Kruass, A. Sayer, and C. Upshurr. 2001. Children with disabilities: A longitudinal study of child development and parent well-being. *Monographs of the Society for Research in Child Development* 66: 1–114.

Hulme, C., K. Goetz, M. Snowling, S. Brigstocke, and H. Nash. 2005. Reading development in children with Down Syndrome: Relationships with oral language and phonological skills. Paper presented at The 4th International Conference on Developmental Issues in Down Syndrome, Portsmouth, UK.

Joffe, V., and S. Varlokosta. 2007. Patterns of syntactic development in children with Williams Syndrome and Down's Syndrome: Evidence from passives and wh-questions. *Clinical Linguistics and Phonetics* 21: 705–727.

Miller, J. 1988. The developmental synchrony of language development in children with Down Syndrome. In *The psychobiology of Down Syndrome*, ed. L. Nadel. Baltimore, MD: Brookes.

Miller, J. 1999. Profiles of language development in children with Down Syndrome. In *Improving the communication of people with Down Syndrome*, ed. J. Miller, M. Leddy, and L. Leavitt. Baltimore, MD: Brookes.

Oelwein, P. 1995. *Teaching reading to your children with Down Syndrome: A guide for parents and teachers*. Bethesda, MD: Woodbine House.

O'Neill, M., and A. Henry. 2002. The grammatical morpheme difficulty in Down Syndrome. *Belfast Working Papers in Language and Linguistics* 15: 65–72.

Price, J., J. Roberts, N. Vandergrift, and G. Martin. 2007. Language comprehension in boys with Fragile X syndrome and boys with Down Syndrome. *Journal of Intellectual Disability* 51: 318–326.

Roizen, N. 2002. Down Syndrome. In *Children with disabilities*, ed. M. Batshaw, 5th ed. Baltimore, MD: Brookes.

Roberts, J., J. Price, and C. Malkin. 2007. Language and communication development in Down Syndrome. *Mental Retardation and Developmental Disabilities Review* 13: 26–35.

Roch, M., and M. Levorato. 2009. Simple view of reading in Down's Syndrome: The role of listening comprehension and reading skills. *International Journal of Language Communication Disorders* 44: 206–223.

Roizen, N., C. Wolters, T. Nicol, and T. Blondis. 1993. Hearing loss in children with Down syndrome. *The Journal of Pediatrics* 123: S9–S12.

Rondal, J. 1995. *Exceptional language development in Down Syndrome*. Cambridge, UK: Cambridge University Press.

Rondal, J. 2006. Specific language profiles in Down Syndrome and other genetic syndromes of mental retardation. In *Down Syndrome: Neurobehavioural specificity*, ed. J. Rondal and J. Perera. Sussex, UK: Wiley.

Rondal, J., and A. Comblain. 1996. Language in adults with Down Syndrome. *Down Syndrome* 4: 3–14.

Rondal, J., and S. Edwards. 1997. *Language in mental retardation*. London, UK: Whurr Publishers.

Rondal, J., and J. Perera, eds. 2006. *Down Syndrome: Neurobehavioral specificity*. Chichester, UK: Wiley.

Schaner-Wolles, C. 2000. Within-language dissociations in mental retardation: Williams-Beuren and Down Syndrome. *Proceedings of the 24th Annual Boston University Conference on Language Development* 2: 633–644.

Seagoe, M. 1965. Verbal development in a mongoloid. *Exceptional Children* 31: 269–273.

Seidl, A., G. Hollich, and P. Jusczyk. 2003. Early understanding of subject and object questions. *Infancy* 4: 423–436.

Shott, S., A. Joseph, and D. Heithaus. 2001. Hearing loss in children with Down Syndrome. *International Journal of Pediatric Otorhinolaryngology* 201: 1999–2205.

Smith, B., and D. Oller. 1981. A comparative study of premeaningful vocalizations produced by normally developing and Down's Syndrome infants. *Journal of Speech and Hearing Disorders* 46: 46–51.

Smith, N., and I.-M. Tsimpli. 1995. *The mind of a savant: Language learning and modularity*. Oxford, UK: Basil Blackwell.

Tew, B. 1979. The "cocktail party syndrome" in children with hydrocephalus and spina bifida. *British Journal of Disorders of Communication* 14: 89–101.

Thordardottir, E., R. Chapman, and L. Wagner. 2002. Complex syntax production by adolescents with Down Syndrome. *Applied Psycholinguistics* 23: 163–183.

Weissenborn, J., B. Hohle, D. Kiefer, and D. Cavar. 1998. Children's sensitivity to word order violations in German: Evidence for very early parameter setting. Proceedings of the 22nd Boston University Conference on Language Development, 756–767. Somerville, MA: Cascadilla Press.

Wisniewski, K., E. Kida, A. Golabek, M. Walus, A. Rabe, S. Palminiello, and G. Albertini. 2006. Down Syndrome: From pathology to pathogenesis. In *Down Syndrome: Neurobehavioural specificity*, ed. J. Rondal and J. Perera. Sussex, UK: Wiley.

Yamada, J. 1990. *Laura: A case for the modularity of language*. Cambridge, MA: MIT Press.

Chapter 2
Ten Syntactic Structures

Abstract We review the structures tested in our comprehension study of syntax in persons with Down Syndrome (DS), arguing them to be mastered over a period between around 2 years and 12 years by typically developing children. The structures are: the simple active and the simple passive; complements to verbs such as *tell* with either a main clause that is active or a main clause that is passive; the complement to the verb *promise*; complements to *eager*- vs. *easy*-type predicates; gerundial (*-ing*) adjunct clauses to main verbs that are either in the active or in the passive voice; and the complement to *choose* type verbs that have a missing object. The order of acquisition by typically developing children is confirmed with a new experiment.

Keywords Simple/complex syntax · Typically developing children · Order of acquisition

2.1 The Structures

We focus on ten English constructions that have been shown to be mastered at different ages in typically developing children: the simple active and the simple passive; complements to verbs such as *tell* verbs with either an active or a passive main clause; the complement to the verb *promise*; complements to *eager*- vs. *easy*-type predicates; gerundial (*-ing*) adjunct clauses to main verbs that are either in the active or in the passive voice; and the complement to *choose* type verbs that have a missing object.

The simple active and passive

By age 3–4, children generally score well above chance on both the active and the passive of action verbs such as *kiss* in (1–2) (for example, Maratsos et al. 1985; Stromswold, n.d.), although more errors are made with the passive.[1]

[1] In this chapter we will be concerned only with the passive of action verbs. See Chap. 5 for discussion of the passive of verbs that do not denote an action (such as verbs of perception).

H. Goodluck, *Complex Syntax in the Language of Persons with Down Syndrome*, SpringerBriefs in Linguistics,
https://doi.org/10.1007/978-3-030-96440-5_2

1. Dad kisses mom
2. Dad is kissed by mom.

Complement to *tell/ask*

Children aged 3–4 in general correctly make the empty subject of the complement to *tell/ask* refer to the object of the main clause when the main clause is active,

3. Paul tells Sue to kiss mom

(e.g. Chomsky 1969; Goodluck 1981; Hsu et al. 1985; McDaniel et al. 1990/1991). When the main clause is passive, the reference of the empty subject shifts to the main clause subject,

4. Sue is told by Paul to kiss mom.

Provided the main clause is interpreted correctly, this is the interpretation 4 year olds give to a sentence such as (4) (Goodluck 1981; Goodluck and Behne 1992).

Complement to *promise*

In a sentence such as (5), with the main verb *promise*, the reference of the embedded clause subject is the main clause subject, contrary to the rule for active sentences with a main verb such as *tell*,

5. Paul promises Sue to kiss mom.

This rule is not adopted until 6–7 years of age (Chomsky 1969; Goodluck 1981; but see Cohen Sherman and Lust 1993), with children generally making the main clause object subject of the embedded clause. Thus *promise* is assimilated to the pattern for active *tell*.

Complement to *eager vs. easy*

In (6) the main clause subject is made subject of the embedded clause, whereas in (7), the main clause subject is made object of the embedded clause and the subject of the embedded clause is interpreted as arbitrary in reference,

6. Sue is eager to kiss
7. Sue is easy to kiss.

Knowledge of the difference between the two classes of predicates is not reliably found until after 7 years (Chomsky 1969; McKee 1997; Anderson 2005), although there may be startling exceptions to that guideline age of acquisition (Cromer 1987). Generally, the child error pattern has been to assimilate the interpretation of sentence type (7) to that of sentence type (6).

Temporal adjunct clauses

Temporal (and other types of) adjunct clauses do not shift their interpretation according to the voice (active vs. passive) of the main clause, in contrast to the complement to *tell*-type verbs. Thus in both (8) and (9), the (surface) main clause subject is interpreted as the subject of the adjunct clause,

8. Paul kisses Sue before leaving the room
9. Sue is kissed by Paul before leaving the room.

A variety of error types have been found in children as old as 7–9 years of age. Children have been found to interpret the agent of the main clause as subject of the subordinate clause (correct for 8, but incorrect for 9), or to treat the embedded subject as arbitrary in reference, allowing either the subject or object, or an entity not mentioned in the sentence, to be interpreted as subject of the embedded clause (Goodluck 1981; Hsu et al. 1985; McDaniel et al. 1990/1991; Goodluck and Behne 1992). See Goodluck (2001) for a summary.

Complement to *choose* with object gap

The interpretation of the complement to verbs such as *choose* follow the pattern of verbs such as *tell*, with a switch from main clause object to main clause subject as referent of the subordinate subject when the main clause is active vs. when the main clause is passive (*Sue chooses Paul to sing* vs. *Sue is chosen by Paul to sing*). *Choose*-type verbs also permit an empty object position. In (10), the subject of the main verb is made subject of the subordinate verb and the object of the main verb is made (prepositional) object of the subordinate one,

10. Sue chooses Paul to sing to.

Children are often as old as 10 years or more before they learn the correct interpretation of sentences such as (10), sometimes being baffled by the preposition at the end ("sing to who?") (Goodluck and Behne 1992; Goodluck 1994).

2.2 The Order of Acquisition

The order in which the structures listed above corresponds (with the exception of *easy* predicates) approximately to the order in which we assume they are mastered, as given in Table 2.1.

We are not claiming that typically developing children are always, for example, 6 years or older before they have any knowledge of the fact that the main clause subject is made subject of the complement of *promise*, or any knowledge that *easy* predicates require the object of the main clause to be made coreferential with the object of the embedded clause; some studies cited above challenge such claims. However, the literature we have cited suggests that the order of acquisition in typically developing children is generally accurate, and this order is confirmed by a study reported in the next section.

Table 2.1 Typical age of acquisition

Construction	Age of acquisition
Active	Below 2 years
Passive	3–4 years
Interpretation of complement to *tell*, with main clause active or passive	3–4 years
Interpretation of complement to *eager*	3–4 years
Interpretation of complement to *promise*	6–7 years
Interpretation of complement to *easy*	7–8 years
Interpretation of temporal adjuncts, with main clause active or passive	7–9 years
Interpretation of object gap in purpose clauses	10+ years

2.3 An Experimental Confirmation of the Order of Acquisition

2.3.1 Participants

The acquisition studies cited above use different methodologies (including act-out with toys, sentence judgement and sentence production). In order to check our assumed order of acquisition was correct, we administered an act-out comprehension test to a group of 31 typically developing children (10 four- to five-year olds, 9 seven- to eight-year olds and 12 ten- to eleven-year olds). These children were recruited in the greater Toronto area from a local school and through personal connections with the researchers. Parents of these children completed a demographic questionnaire and a brief developmental history questionnaire to ensure normal development. All the children were enrolled in regular classrooms and had not repeated any grades. The children did the test in two sessions (either with a lunch-time break in between or on two separate days).

2.3.2 Task and Experimental Materials

The task used was act-out: the enactment of sentences read by the experimenter to the child. The props for the act-out consisted of a doll family (mom, dad, and two children) and a number of pets/small objects (a cat, a rabbit, a fence, a wall, and a wooden block). The names of each child (Paul and Sue) were taught at the beginning of the session, and were printed in 16 pt. typeface on labels affixed to the doll's chest. The sentences to be acted out consisted of six tokens each of simple active and passive sentences (1–2), and four tokens each of the remaining sentences types (3–10). The materials were arranged so that simple active and passive sentences were roughly evenly distributed through the questionnaire, and the more challenging (later acquired) constructions (8–10) were introduced in the second and third sections of the questionnaire. A complete set of the sentences is given in Appendix 1. A sentence was repeated up to two times if the child did not respond on first presentation.

2.3.3 *Results*

The typically developing children performed as we expected based on the previous literature. Figure 2.1 gives the mean correct responses for each age group.

In Table 2.2 we analyse the performance of individual children. A child was classed as a 'passer' if he or she had 75% or more correct responses for a sentence type (4/6 for sentence types 1 and 2 and 3/4 for sentence types 3–10). As Table 2.2 shows, the 10–11 year olds all score as passers for all sentence types except (9) and (10). For 4–5 year olds, the lowest numbers of passers were for sentence type 5 (*promise*), and sentence types 7–10 (*easy*, temporal complements and *choose*). The proportions of 7–8 year olds fall in between those of the youngest and oldest children for sentence types 5, 7, 9 and 10. Chi-square tests on the distribution of passers by age group are significant for *promise* (Chi-square = 11.74, $p = < 0.005$) and for *easy* (Chi-square = 8.32, $p < 0.02$) and approached significance for temporal passive and *choose* ($p < 0.10 > 0.05$ in both cases).

We examined the response pattern for individual subjects for *eager/easy* constructions and for temporal adjunct conditions. The predicates we used in our test of *eager/easy* comprised *eager, glad, keen,* and *happy* vs. *easy, hard, fun,* and *tough.* Of the object gap predicates, only one individual lexical item stood out: the predicate *hard* was responded to more successfully (with 8 out of 10 4–5 *year* olds correctly interpreting it) than the other object gap predicates *tough, easy and fun* (with 1 child, 2 and 4 children respectively giving correct responses). This is consistent with the findings of McKee (1997), who found that *hard* was the most successfully interpreted of the predicates she studied for 4 and 5 year olds.

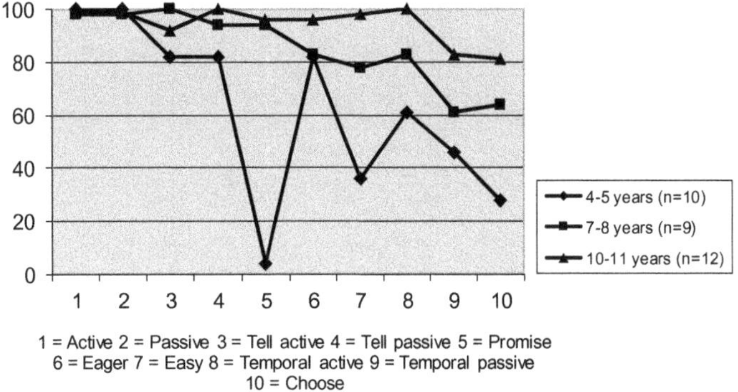

Fig. 2.1 Mean percentage correct: typically developing children

Table 2.2 Number of typically developing children with 75% or more correct by syntactic structure and age

		Structure									
		1	2	3	4	5	6	7	8	9	10
		Active	Passive	Tell active	Tell passive	Promise	Eager	Easy	Temp active	Temp passive	Choose
Age	4–5 years ($n = 10$)	10	9	8	6	0	8	2	5	3	2
	7–8 years ($n = 9$)	9	9	9	8	8	9	5	9	6	6
	10–11 years ($n = 12$)	12	12	12	12	12	12	12	12	11	10

For the temporal adjunct conditions, we could identify only two clear incorrect patterns in our data: the tendency to treat the agent of the main clause as PRO, correct for the active condition and incorrect for the passive (3 subjects in the 4–5 age group, and 1 in the 7–8 age group); and the tendency to treat the patient of the main clause as PRO (2 subjects in the 4–5 age group). The patient pattern has not clearly been identified in previous studies. The criterion used for the classification was 3 or 4 responses of a particular type, or 2/3 responses if the child had only three responses in which the main and subordinate clauses were correctly acted out; by this criterion 2 children had adult responses in the 4–5 age group, 8 children in the 7–8 group and 11 children in the 10–11 group. The remaining children (3 in the 4–5 age group, and 1 in the 10–11 group) did not show any clear non-adult or adult pattern.

2.4 Causes of Development

What makes the grammar of the typical child develop? We will assume that the child comes to language acquisition equipped with knowledge of Universal Grammar (UG)—that is, that s/he has unconscious knowledge of the fact that, for example, human languages can involve structures with 'missing' subjects and objects, that c-command (see below) regulates the reference of some missing entities, and that human languages may have a passive operation of some kind. The task for the child is to work out what the realization of such entities is, and the rules that apply to them are, in the particular grammar that s/he is exposed to.

There two primary candidates for an explanation of the order in which a construction is acquired, which may work together to affect the speed of acquisition: input frequency and complexity of the structure to be acquired. The latter may affect not merely the point at which the child acquires the basic knowledge of a structure, but may affect his/her ability to use that knowledge in real time (for example, to act out the utterance).

For all the sentence types tested, there has been extensive—and in some cases inconclusive—debate in the theoretical literature concerning their correct characterization. What follows is a traveller's guide to that literature. In many cases we ignore hot debates, but we hope to give a general impression of what is at stake for the constructions tested.

Simple active and passive sentences

We know from studies such as Hirsch-Pasek and Golinkoff (1996) that the basic word order of active sentences such as (1) is recognised at the earliest stage that at present we can experimentally test. For example, these researchers found that infants as young as 16–19 months look longer at videotapes accompanied by word strings that conform to the basic Subject Verb Object than videos that violated that order (videos in which the wrong entity was subject of the action depicted). That is, infants recognise the basic word order of active sentences at an age when they produce only one or two word utterances.

When do children first acquire the more complex sentence type (2), the passive? Theoretical analyses differ as to whether and how the subject of an active sentence becomes the object of the *by* phrase in the passive, but most analyses agree that the object of an active sentence is moved to subject position by the operation of forming the passive,

11. Dad_i is kissed t_i

(The *t* in 11 stands for trace, a phonetically empty element left by a movement operation.)[2] Thus a passive sentence offers the challenge for the learner of understanding that the object (*patient* or *theme*) occupies the subject position, rather than the subject being occupied by the *agent*, as is the case for action verbs, and that the agent in the passive of an action verb is expressed in a *by* phrase. A difference between active and passive sentences in adult sentence processing has been recognised since studies such as Forster and Olbrei (1973), with passive sentences taking longer to comprehend.[3]

The passive of verbs is much less frequent in the input to children than the active, as is the occurrence of the passive with a *by* phrase (see Nguyen and Pearl 2017 for an overview). Despite this relatively impoverished input, English-speaking children as young as less than two years produce some passives; all of the 13 children studied by Snyder and Stromswold (1997) produced passives before the turn of their third year. Nguyen and Pearl argue that the frequency of occurrence of the passive cannot account for the speed with which children acquire the passive, but rather that lexical semantic features can do so, with action verbs leading the way. But nonetheless children as old as five or six perform less well in understanding passives than in understanding active sentences. Stromswold (n.d.) argues that passive sentences offer a challenge to the sentence processing device, despite the grammar of passives being mature. This is scarcely a surprising conclusion, given the fact that studies from Forster and Olbrei onwards argue that in adult sentence processing the passive requires more energy (takes more time) than processing the active.

Four sentence types with an embedded PRO clause

There are two pairs of sentences in our battery that involve active vs. passive main clauses and embedded clauses with an unpronounced subject: (3–4) with a main verb such as *tell* (exemplified by *tell* and *ask*) and (8–9), with action verbs in the main clause and a subordinate adjunct clause.

---

[2] There is another construction in English: the adjectival passive. We will not be concerned with the adjectival passive here, but see, for example, Goodluck (2020) for a brief summary of the acquisition literature.

[3] At the time of publication of Forster and Olbrei's article, it was a controversial matter whether the difficulty of passive sentences only applied to sentences that offered no pragmatic clue to their correct analysis (*reversible* passives such as that in 2, in which the subject and object can be exchanged, as opposed to *non-reversible* passives, such as *The flowers were watered by the girl,* in which such exchange yields a semantically bizarre sentence). See Forster and Olbrei for discussion.

In the case of *tell*-type sentences, the main verb is specified to allow the inclusion of an embedded (complement) clause. In the case of sentences with adjunct clauses, there is no restriction imposed by the main verb—a temporal adjunct clause can occur with any verb. For both the complement to *tell*-type verbs and adjunct clauses in our test, the subject of the subordinate verb is not overt. The subject position is designated with an unpronounced element, PRO, the reference of which is determined by rules of grammar. Although it is a controversial matter how the rules for PRO are formulated (see, for example, Radford 2004, pp. 91–107, 238–241, and references therein), the results are quite clear for these cases. In the case of complements to *tell*, it is the patient (theme) of the main verb that is made referent of the empty element PRO; and in the case of adjunct clauses, it is the surface subject of the main clause that is made to co-refer with PRO.

12.a Paul tells Sue [PRO to kiss mom]

12.b Sue is told by Paul [PRO to kiss mom]

13.a Paul kisses Sue [before PRO leaving the room]

13.b Sue is kissed by Paul [before PRO leaving the room]

There is a difference in the overall structure of complement and adjunct clauses, the former being within the verb phrase and the latter higher in the structure outside the verb phrase,[4]

14.a Structure for complement to V
Main clause active

14.b Structure for complement to V
Main clause passive

[4] IP (Inflectional Phrase) has replaced S (Sentence) in the linguistic literature over the past 30 years. IP is generally considered an abbreviation for a cluster of nodes which specify the tense and aspect of the verb. In the interest of making the explanation of c-command in (16) below simpler, the trees in (14–15) include tertiary branching. Such branching is eschewed in current linguistic literature, but the generalization concerning c-command and PRO is not affected.

15. Structure for temporal adjuncts
Main clause active or passive

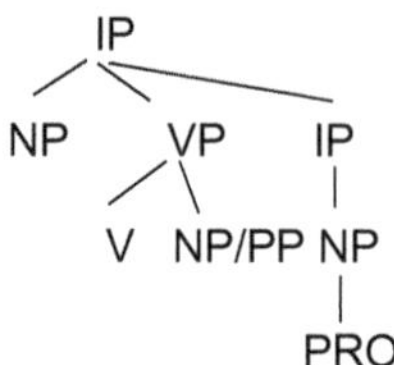

A generalization can be made with respect to the reference of PRO in (12–13): the PRO must be c-commanded by the noun phrase it refers to. The relation c-command (constituent-command) is a basic relation that is evident in many areas of grammar:

16. C-command: Node A c-commands node B if and only if the first branching node also dominates A and neither A nor B c-command the other.

In (12a) both the subject of the main verb and the object of the main verb c-command PRO because the first branching node (IP in the case of the subject and VP in the case of the object) also dominates PRO. A further specification in terms of the role of the NP that refers to PRO is needed—it is the patient role of the verb.

In both (13a) and (13b), because the embedded clause is attached high in the structure (15), it is the subject of the main clause that PRO refers to.

We have assumed that children come equipped with a basic knowledge that includes c-command and its strictures, and the existence PRO, but children need exposure to the language to learn which structures PRO belongs in. For active *tell* sentences, it is plausible to surmise that a child hears sentences such as 'I told you to jump in the bath!', giving him/her a clue that the patient co-refers with the empty subject of the embedded clause. And indeed children do very well with sentences of type (12a). Given our assumptions about c-command and PRO, we also assume that a child will do well with passive sentences such as (12b), and again this is correct, if the main clause is correctly interpreted as passive.

In the case of sentence types (8–9 = 13a–13b), with a temporal adjunct clause, children struggle. Their struggle is with the interpretation on the PRO subject of the embedded clause rather than with the interpretation of the passive. As noted above, children display various misinterpretations of the PRO in adjuncts, which are at times systematic. In our sample of typically developing children, we saw that some children systematically interpret PRO as referring to the agent of the main clause and others the patient of the main clause, and well as making non-systematic misinterpretations of PRO until age 8.

Tensed temporal clauses occur in very early child speech. However, gerundial adjuncts of the type in (8–9) are vanishingly rare in the input data (Broihier and Wexler 1995) and the child may not be familiar with such structures until s/he begins to read. So what is the source of the at-times systematic, but non-adult interpretations of sentences such as (8–9)? We know from studies in other areas of grammar (particularly pronoun interpretation) that children have some grasp of the fact that adjunct clauses are attached to the syntactic structure at a position outside the VP (see, for example, Solan 1983). And so it would seem that at least some patterns of interpretation violate the restriction that PRO can only refer to a c-commanding NP.

A solution to the manner in which children handle gerundive adjunct clauses without violation of this principle of grammar was suggested by Carlson (1991), and some experimental support for Carlson's hypothesis was provided by Goodluck (2001). Carlson's idea was that children use a structure along the lines in (17b), in lieu of the correct structure in (17a),

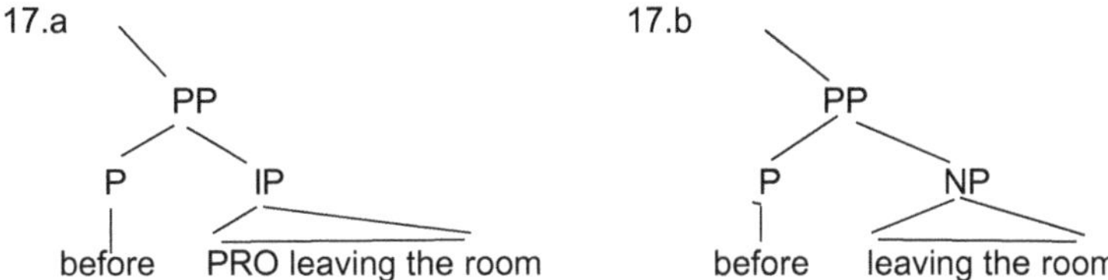

That is, children employ a nominal structure, in which PRO is not present. The interpretation of the subject position of a nominal structure is characteristically free in grammars, and thus children's range of interpretations can be accounted for under Carlson's hypothesis. The experimental evidence that Goodluck provided comes from the interpretation of *by*-phrases inside the gerundial adjunct clause. The preposition *by* is ambiguous between a locative and agentive reading. In the adult grammar, a *by*-phrase can only be interpreted as agentive if embedded within a nominal structure. Thus (18a) contrasts with (18b), in that only (18b) permits an agentive reading of the *by*-phrase,

18.a Pluto pushes Champion before PRO hopping by Daisy
[Locative interpretation of *by* obligatory; agentive reading of the object of *by* is blocked]

18.b Pluto pushes Champion before some hopping by Daisy
[Agentive reading of the object of *by* permitted]

The PRO subject of (18a) must be assigned the thematic [semantic] role agent, and hence the agent role cannot be assigned to *Daisy* (there cannot be two identical thematic roles in the same clause).

Four to six year old children in Goodluck's study freely permitted an agentive reading of the *by* phrase in sentences such as (18a), something that adults never did, arguing in favour of the nominalization account of children's errors.,[5,6]

More PRO sentences: Lexical restrictions and sentences with empty objects
There are four constructions that we have not dealt with yet: The complement to *promise,* the complements to *easy* and *eager* type predicates, and the complement to *choose*-type verbs with an object gap.

We can see from Fig. 2.1 that there is an abrupt shift for *promise* from age 4–5 to age 6–7: children almost always get the interpretation of *promise* wrong at 4–5 (with the embedded PRO almost always interpreted as object, not subject, of the main verb), and right at age 6–7. What causes this shift? It seems implausible that the input varies much between the two ages. A common explanation has been that the child frees him/herself from an overgeneralization from *tell*-type verbs that the patient of the main clause is made referent of the PRO in the subordinate clause, although what causes this change remains obscure.

What about *eager* vs. *easy* constructions? In the *easy* construction, there is a phonetically null subordinate object position in addition to an empty subject position. A frequent proposal in the linguistic literature is that null object constructions are formed by moving a phonetically null operator to a slot (CP, the Complementizer Phrase) at the front of the embedded clause,

19. Sue is easy [$_{CP}$ [PRO to kiss O] = >
Sue is easy [$_{CP}$ O_i [PRO to kiss t_i]

The use of a movement operation for these constructions is controversial (see, for example, Jones 1987), but is still widely accepted (see, for example, Botwinik-Rotem 2008). This movement leaves no clue on the surface of the sentence—unlike the passive, which is marked by morphology (*was/is* V-*ed*). The *eager* construction, by contrast, involves no movement and no empty object position. The error made by children is overwhelmingly to interpret the *easy* construction as an *eager* construction, with no movement operation. Children presumably rely on the presence of obligatory (or near obligatory) transitive verbs in the embedded clause to establish which predicates fall in the *easy* class. On the evidence of this and many other studies, this process may take into the school years.

Finally, we have the complement to *choose*-type verbs with an empty object position (sentence type 10). This too is analysed as involving the movement of a phonetically null operator into the complementizer phrase, coindexing the subject

---

[5] It should be noted that the hypothesis that children treat PRO constructions in the adult grammar as nominalizations can account for the range of different interpretations reported in the literature, but cannot account for why particular interpretations are used from one study to the next. To date, this is unexplained.

[6] Landau (2021) presents an analysis in terms of whether the adjunct clause is optionally or obligatorily controlled. We leave it as an open question as to whether this alternative can account for the acquisition facts.

of the main clause with PRO, and coindexing the object of the main clause with the operator,

20. Sue chooses Paul [$_{CP}$ [PRO to read to O] = >
Sue$_i$ chooses Paul$_j$ [$_{CP}$ O$_j$ [PRO$_i$ to read to t$_j$]

The main verbs used in our test were *choose* and *pick* and the empty position was unambiguously signalled by an obligatorily transitive preposition. Despite the presence of the empty preposition, only two children in the youngest age group tested scored 3 or 4 correct, six children at age 7–8 scored 3 or 4 correct, and even in the oldest group two children failed to reach that level, confirming that it was the most difficult of the constructions we tested.

2.5 Summary and Conclusion

The constructions that we tested are challenging for the child on a number of different grounds: their derivation may involve movement (in the case of passive, with movement to subject position, and *easy* predicates and *choose* predicates, with 'invisible' movement of an operator); and they require in all cases except temporal adjuncts knowledge of the mapping between individual lexical items and syntactic structure. Moreover, the input to the child may not offer frequent exemplars of the construction at hand. The typically developing child masters the constructions we tested by around 8 years, with the possible exception of temporal adjuncts and the *choose* construction. In the next chapter, we compare the performance of individuals with Down Syndrome against these timelines for acquisition.

References

Anderson, D. 2005. The acquisition of tough-movement in English. PhD dissertation, University of Cambridge, UK.

Botwinik-Rotem, I. 2008. Object gap constructions: Externalization and operator movement. In *Current issues in Hebrew linguistics*, ed. S. Armon-Lotem, G. Danon and S. Rothestein. Amsterdam, The Netherlands: John Benjamins.

Broihier, K., and K. Wexler. 1995. Children's acquisition of control in temporal adjuncts. *MIT Working Papers in Linguistics* 26: 193–220.

Carlson, G. 1991. Intuitions, category and structure: Comments on McDaniel and Cairns. In *Language acquisition and language processing*, ed. L. Frazier and J. de Villiers, 327–333. Dordrecht, The Netherlands: Kluwer.

Chomsky, C. 1969. *The acquisition of syntax in children from 5 to 10.* Cambridge, MA: MIT Press.

Cohen Sherman, J., and B. Lust. 1993. Children are in control. *Cognition* 43: 1–51.

Cromer, R. 1987. Language growth with experience without feedback. *Journal of Psycholinguistic Research* 16: 223–232.

Forster, K., and I. Olbrei. 1973. Semantic heuristics and syntactic analysis. *Cognition* 2: 319–347.

Goodluck, H. 1981. Children's grammar of complement subject interpretation. In *Language acquisition and linguistic theory*, ed. S. Tavakolian. Cambridge, MA: MIT Press.

Goodluck, H. 1994. Current grammars vs. rule-based guessing in children's interpretation of some complex sentence types. In *The reality of linguistic rules*, ed. R. Corrigan, G. Iverson, and S. Lima, 221–242. Amsterdam, Holland: John Benjamins.

Goodluck, H. 2001. The nominal analysis of children's interpretation of adjunct PRO clauses. *Language* 77: 494–509.

Goodluck, H. 2020. *Language acquisition by children: A linguistic introduction.* Edinburgh, UK: Edinburgh University Press.

Goodluck, H., and D. Behne. 1992. Development in control and extraction. In *Theoretical issues in language acquisition*, ed. J. Weissenborn, H. Goodluck, and T. Roeper. Hillsdale, NJ: Lawrence Erlbaum Associates.

Hirsh-Pasek, K., and R. Golinkoff. 1996. *The origins of grammar: Evidence from early child comprehension.* Cambridge, MA: MIT Press.

Hsu, J., H. Cairns, and R. Fiengo. 1985. The development of grammars underlying children's complex sentences. *Cognition* 20: 25–48.

Jones, C. 1987. *Purpose clauses: Syntax, thematics and semantics of English purpose constructions.* Dordrecht, The Netherlands: Kluwer Academic Publishers.

Landau, I. 2021. *A selectional theory of adjunct control.* Cambridge, MA: MIT Press.

Maratsos, M., D. Fox, J. Becker, and M. Chalkley. 1985. Semantic restrictions on children's passives. *Cognition* 19: 167–191.

McDaniel, D., H. Cairns, and J. Hsu. 1990/1991. Control principles in the grammars of young children. *Language Acquisition* 1: 297–335.

McKee, C. 1997. Some adjectives are 'easy' and some are not. *Lexicology* 3: 59–83.

Nguyen, E., and L. Pearl. 2017. Do you really mean it? Linking lexical semantic profiles and age of acquisition for the English passive. In *Proceedings of the 35th west coast conference on formal linguistics*, ed. W. Bennett, L. Hracs, and D. Storoshenko, 288–295. Somerville, MA: Cascadilla Proceedings Project.

Radford, A. 2004. *English syntax: An introduction.* Cambridge, UK: Cambridge University Press.

Snyder, W., and K. Stromswold. 1997. The structure and acquisition of English dative constructions. *Linguistic Inquiry* 28: 281–312.

Solan, L. 1983. *Pronominal reference: Child language and the theory of grammar.* Dordrecht, The Netherlands: Reidel.

Stromswold, K. n.d. Ms. Rutgers University.

Chapter 3
Aural and Written Comprehension by Persons with Down Syndrome

Abstract We report the results of tests of comprehension in persons with Down Syndrome (DS) of the 10 syntactic structures reviewed in Chap. 2: simple active sentences; simple passive sentences; active *tell* sentences with an infinitival complement; passive *tell* sentences with an infinitival complement; active *promise* sentences with an infinitival complement; sentences with the predicate *eager* and an infinitival complement; sentences with the predicate *easy* with an infinitival complement; gerundial temporal clauses with an active main clause; gerundial temporal clauses with a passive main clause; and active sentences with the main verb *choose* and an infinitival complement with a missing prepositional object. The tests used were an act-out test with a doll family and a written test in which the participant had to choose between two answers. The participants were persons with DS who could read (25 participants for the act-out and 24 for the written test). A comparison between typically developing children aged 4 to 12 shows an overall similarity between when the structures are acquired by children and persons with DS. However, a comparable leap in performance of typically developing children between ages 4–5 and 7–8 for *promise* is not found for persons with DS. Despite this, the results of the act-out test for persons with DS show a significant difference in the direction of knowledge of English grammar between *tell* active and *promise*. There are also significant differences consistent with English grammar between *tell* active and *tell* passive and *eager* vs. *easy* sentences. No significant differences between these sentence types were found for the written test, although the difference between *eager* and *easy* for some participants is stronger for the written test than for the act-out test. Also in the written test, there were more patterned responses to gerundial temporal clauses. A preference for reference of the embedded null subject of active *tell* sentences to the linearly nearest NP can account for a higher performance on the written test than the act-out.

Keywords Standardized tests · Act-out comprehension · Written comprehension · Paired comparisons of PRO structures

H. Goodluck, *Complex Syntax in the Language of Persons with Down Syndrome*, SpringerBriefs in Linguistics,
https://doi.org/10.1007/978-3-030-96440-5_3

3.1 The Structures Tested

The ten syntactic structures reviewed in Chap. 2 (repeated in Sect. 3.3.1) were studied in two tests: an act-out comprehension test and a written test. To our knowledge, with the exception of studies of the simple active and passive by Bridges and Smith (1984), Rubin (2006), Joffe and Varlokosta (2007) and Miolo et al. (2005), none of these constructions has been the focus of previous studies of syntactic knowledge in persons with DS.

3.2 Participants

Twenty-five individuals with DS were tested in the Ottawa-Carleton and Toronto metropolitan regions of Ontario, Canada. Their chronological age ranged from 8 to 33 years at first testing. Inclusion criteria for individuals with DS were: parental/caregiver reports of an ability to read at the sentence level, reasonably intelligible speech, and no ongoing hearing difficulties or recurrent episodes of otitis media in the last five years, defined as four or more episodes in a single year. An additional four participants were recruited but were excluded from the study at the time of intake. Three of these participants had insufficient language and reading abilities to carry out the tasks used in our study, and one had a moderate hearing loss for which he wore hearing aids.

Participants with DS were given three standardized tests: The Peabody Picture Vocabulary Test, Third Edition (PPVT-3) (Dunn and Dunn 1997), the Test of Aural Comprehension of Language Revised (TACL-R) (Carrow-Woolfolk 1985) and the Gates MacGinitie Reading Comprehension Test (MacGinitie and MacGinitie 1989). Participants or their caretakers selected an applicable reading subtest from among the five levels of the Gates MacGinitie, based on their reading ability. Parents/caregivers of the participants with DS also completed a questionnaire concerning the socio-economic profile of the household and the reading practices they had used with their children at younger ages.[1] Scores on the standardized tests are given in Appendix 1.

[1] Household income level was not declared for three of the participants. We divided the remaining participants according to household income level at first testing, and used that grouping to compare both chronological age and age equivalence on the Peabody Picture Vocabulary Test.

	Chronological	PPVT
	Age (in months)	Age (in months)
>$60,000 (n = 14)	244.14	99.71
<$60,000 (n = 8)	213.75	71.25

The mean chronological age of the participants in each group did not differ (t-test, 2 tail, $p > 0.5$); the means for the PPVT did differ (t-test, 2 tail, $p < 0.006$).

We did not measure mental age of our participants. Many persons in the community of parents/carers of individuals with DS in the locations where we tested feel that mental age testing is not appropriate. Although not considered interchangeable with mental age scores, scores on the PPVT have been found to correlate positively with standard intelligence tests such as the Wechsler Intelligence Scale for Children, Third Edition (Wechsler 1991). PPVT-III correlations with WISC-III Verbal IQ are 0.91 (PPVT version IIIA) and 0.92 (PPVT version IIIB).

3.3 Comprehension Tests

The battery of standardized and purpose made tests was administered to our DS participants over three sessions lasting approximately 1.5 hours each. Each session was comprised of part of the standardised tests and part of the purpose made tests.

3.3.1 Act-Out Comprehension

In this test, participants acted out their understanding of sentence types (1–10), listed here again for convenience of reference. The materials were identical to those used for testing typically developing children, as given in Appendix 2, with six tokens of the simple active and passive sentences and four tokens of the remaining sentence types.

1. Simple active sentences
   Mom kisses Dad
2. Simple passive sentences
   Dad is kissed by Mom
3. Complement to *tell/ask*: main clause active
   Sue tells Paul to kiss Mom
4. Complement to *tell/ask*: main clause passive
   Sue is told by Paul to kiss Mom
5. Complement to *promise*
   Sue promises Paul to kiss Mom
6. *eager* predicates
   Sue is eager to kiss
7. *easy* predicates
   Sue is easy to kiss
8. Temporal adjunct clause: main clause active
   Sue kisses Mom before jumping over the fence
9. Temporal adjunct clause: main clause passive
   Sue is kissed by Mom before jumping over the fence

10. Complement to *choose* with a prepositional object gap
    Sue chooses Paul to read to.

After the experimenter taught the participant how to act out sentences using simple active sentences, the participant went on to the main test battery. As for the typically developing children, the names of the two child dolls were printed on labels affixed to the doll's chest. And also as for the typically developing children, the sentences were read to them by the experimenter, and were repeated up to two times if the participant did not at first respond.

3.3.2 Act-Out Results

Simple correlations between correct performance by participants with DS on each of the constructions in (1–10) and performance on the standardized tests showed a higher correlation between simple passive and PPVT than for the TACL (PPVT: $r = 0.58$, $p < 0.003$; TACL: $p > 0.10$). As noted above, the participants with DS did not all do the same version of the Gates MacGinitie test, which has different levels of difficulty. The correlations were based on the participant's Grade Equivalence score for the test. As in the case of the TACL, the correlation with simple passive was not significant ($p > 0.09$). No other correlations with any test were significant, except for the correlation between (3) and the TACL sentence subtest ($r = 0.60$, $p < 0.002$), between (9) and all three tests (PPVT: $r = 0.53$, $p < 0.006$; TACL: $r = 0.50$, $p < 0.01$; Gates MacGinitie: $r = 0.49$, $p < 0.02$) and between (10) and the TACL word subtest and Gates MacGinitie Grade Equivalence (TACL: $r = 0.59$, $p < 0.002$; Gates MacGinitie: $r = 0.49$, $p < 0.02$).[2]

When the DS participants are grouped by age equivalence to the controls on the PPVT, there are eight in the 4–5 age equivalence range, twelve in the 7–8 range, and five individuals in the 10–11 age range. These groups were established after nine individuals whose scores did not fall into one of these bands were absorbed into the nearest band. With this grouping, the pattern of performance and development for the typically developing children and persons with DS shows some similarities, although the overall level of success is lower for the participants with DS (Figs. 2.1 and 3.1). In particular, levels of performance on temporal active and passive conditions echoed the pattern for age-related performance by typically developing children. The same analysis of individual responses for the typically developing group was carried out. With the exception of simple active sentences, for which all 25 DS participants reached the criterion of 75% or more correct, and *eager* sentences, for which 21 out of 25 participants reached criterion, the number of participants reaching criterion in any given condition did not exceed 11; Chi-square analyses were therefore not carried out. Five participants reached criterion on conditions 1, 2 and 3, of whom one reached criterion on all conditions except 10.

[2] Given the total number of correlations performed, these significance levels should be treated with caution.

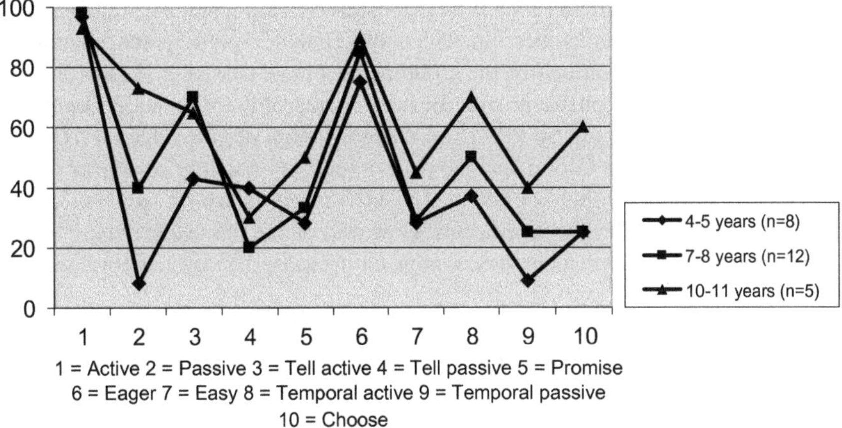

Fig. 3.1 Act-out test mean percentage correct: DS grouped by PPVT equivalents

3.3.2.1 Further Analyses

We made an alternative grouping of the DS participants, based on their performance on the simple passive. This is shown in Fig. 3.2. The grouping by simple passive placed those with no correct responses on simple passive in the Low Group, those with between 16 and 66% correct in the Intermediate group, and those with 67% or more correct in the Upper group. As can be seen from Fig. 3.2, there was a large gap between the Intermediate and the Upper Groups. With one exception the Upper Group all had 100% correct on simple passive, whereas the mean for the Intermediate Group was only 25%. When we compare the membership of the Low, Intermediate

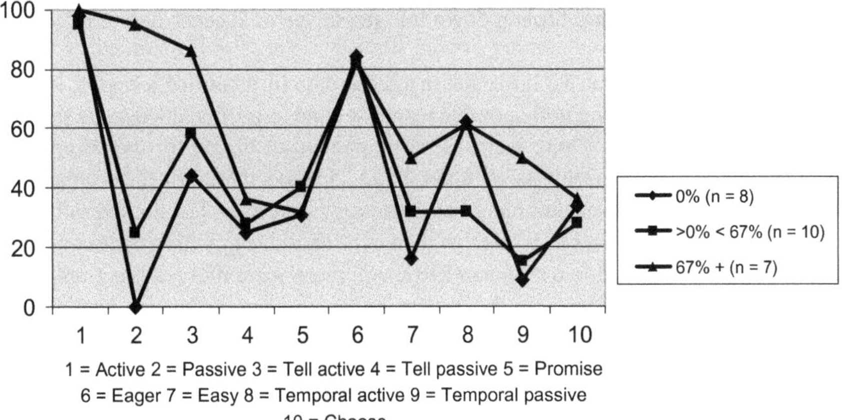

Fig. 3.2 Act-out test mean percentage correct: DS grouped by success on simple passive

and Upper Groups based on PPVT with that based on simple passive, there is a good deal of shifting in group membership, with only 12 out of 25 participants remaining in the same group. Observationally, the grouping by simple passive gives a profile that in some ways is more consistent with the age-based profile for typically developing children than the grouping by PPVT: i.e. there is a high performance on *tell* active sentences for the Upper Group, and the pattern for *eager* vs. *easy* sentences follows that for typically developing children, with high performance on *eager* predicates and a staged pattern for *easy* predicates. However, on the passive grouping there is less differentiation between the three groups for the more difficult temporal sentence types and for *choose*.

As described in Chap. 2, the test constructions (3–10) all involve the interpretation of the phonetically null subject (PRO) of an embedded clause. In order to examine how our participants did in interpreting PRO for pairs of constructions that differ by only one factor, we calculated the number of *scorable* responses for each subject for each condition. We treated a response as scorable if the actions of the main and subordinate clause were acted out correctly, aside from any error in interpreting PRO. For example, if an act-out involved treating a passive main clause as if it were active, this would be classed as unscorable, since it provides no information about the effect of passivization on the interpretation of PRO.

We made four comparisons of the number of Subject vs. Object responses for the scorable data: *tell* active vs. *tell* passive; *tell* active vs. *promise*; *eager* vs. *easy*; and temporal adjunct active vs. temporal adjunct passive. A subject response was a response in which the surface subject of the main clause was made to refer to PRO; and an object response was one in which the (direct or prepositional) object of the main clause was made to refer to PRO. Participants were only included in the analysis if they had at least one scorable response for each of the paired conditions.

In each of the first three comparisons, we found a significant difference in the direction of knowledge of the grammar of English. These results are presented in Tables 3.1, 3.2 and 3.3, which give the overall totals for each comparison and the totals when the results are broken down into the levels of success on the PPVT and the simple passive.

It should be clear that we have massaged the data in favour of a higher level of performance by excluding non-scorable responses and requiring at least one scorable response per condition. There were 18 participants (out of 25) for the comparison between *tell* active and *tell* passive, and 24 and 25 respectively for the comparisons between *tell* active and *promise* and between *eager* and *easy*. For the overall totals, there were more responses to *tell* active than to *tell* passive in which the main clause object was correctly made to refer to PRO, and there were more subject responses to *promise* than to *tell* active. In the case of *eager* vs. *easy* there were overall more responses in which the subject of the main clause was interpreted as object of the embedded predicate for *easy* than for *eager*, again consistent with a knowledge of English grammar.

Some further commentary is needed on the levels established by the PPVT and by success on the simple passive. Neither of these groupings stood out as clearly superior to the other. Although the levels of performance did not reach significance

Table 3.1 Down Syndrome participants: Scorable responses *Tell* active vs. *Tell* passive

Overall performance (n = 18)

	Number of responses	
	Subject[a]	Object[b]
Tell-A	13	43
Tell-P	26	13

[a]Correct for *tell*-P
[b]Correct for *tell*-A
Fisher's exact, p < .000

Grouped by PPVT

Level 1 (n = 6)

	Number of responses	
	Subject	Object
Tell-A	3	13
Tell-P	10	6

Fisher's exact, p < .02

Level 2 (n = 9)

	Number of responses	
	Subject	Object
Tell-A	7	22
Tell-P	10	5

Fisher's exact, p < .001

Level 3 (n = 3)

	Number of responses	
	Subject	Object
Tell-A	3	8
Tell-P	6	2

Fisher's exact, n.s. p < .07

Grouped by passive

Level 1 (n = 6)

	Number of responses	
	Subject	Object
Tell-A	5	9
Tell-P	8	6

Fisher's exact, n.s.

Level 2 (n = 7)

	Number of responses	
	Subject	Object
Tell-A	6	17
Tell-P	8	6

Fisher's exact, n.s. (p < .09)

Level 3 (n = 5)

	Number of responses	
	Subject	Object
Tell-A	2	17
Tell-P	10	1

Fisher's exact, p < .000

Table 3.2 Down Syndrome participants: Scorable responses *Tell* active vs. *Promise*

Overall performance (n = 24)

	Number of responses	
	Subject[a]	Object[b]
Tell	14	61
Promise	33	47

[a]Correct for *promise*
[b]Correct for *tell*
Fisher's exact, p < .007

Grouped by PPVT

Level 1 (n = 7)

	Number of responses	
	Subject	Object
Tell	3	14
Promise	7	16

Fisher's exact, n.s.

Level 2 (n = 12)

	Number of responses	
	Subject	Object
Tell	7	34
Promise	16	23

Fisher's exact, p < .03

Level 3 (n = 5)

	Number of responses	
	Subject	Object
Tell	4	14
Promise	10	8

Fisher's exact, n.s., p < .09

Grouped by passive

Level 1 (n = 8)

	Number of responses	
	Subject	Object
Tell	5	14
Promise	10	16

Fisher's exact, n.s.

Level 2 (n = 9)

	Number of responses	
	Subject	Object
Tell	7	23
Promise	14	13

Fisher's exact, n.s. (p < .07)

Level 3 (n = 7)

	Number of responses	
	Subject	Object
Tell	2	24
Promise	9	18

Fisher's exact, p < .05

Table 3.3 Down Syndrome participants: Scorable responses *Eager* vs. *Easy*

Overall performance (n = 25)

	Number of responses	
	Subject[a]	Object[b]
Eager	81	18
Easy	68	31

[a]Correct for *eager*
[b]Correct for *easy*
Fisher's exact, $p < .05$

Grouped by PPVT

Level 1 (n = 9)

	Number of responses	
	Subject	Object
Eager	29	7
Easy	28	8

Fisher's exact, n.s.

Level 2 (n = 11)

	Number of responses	
	Subject	Object
Eager	36	7
Easy	29	14

Fisher's exact, n.s.

Level 3 (n = 5)

	Number of responses	
	Subject	Object
Eager	16	4
Easy	11	9

Fisher's exact, n.s.

Grouped by passive

Level 1 (n = 8)

	Number of responses	
	Subject	Object
Eager	27	5
Easy	27	5

Fisher's exact, n.s.

Level 2 (n = 10)

	Number of responses	
	Subject	Object
Eager	32	7
Easy	27	12

Fisher's exact, n.s.

Level 3 (n = 7)

	Number of responses	
	Subject	Object
Eager	22	6
Easy	14	14

Fisher's exact, $p < .05$

Table 3.4 Act-out task Performance of two individuals consistent with use of an agent/patient strategy

	Temporal Active			Temporal Passive		
Response:	S	O	NS	S	O	NS
# 2 (agent)	3	0	1	0	2	2
# 8 (patient)	0	1	3	4	0	0

S = (Surface) Subject response
O = (Surface) Object response
NS = Non-scorable response

at each individual level in the analysis, the trends in the data at each level contributed to the significance levels for the overall performance. This is most evident in the data for *eager* vs. *easy*, where the only significant difference was at level 3 in the passive grouping, but the overall performance was significant at the 0.05 level.

For temporal adjunct active vs. passive, for which the correct response for both conditions was for the main clause subject to be made to refer to PRO, there were 17 individuals who had at least one scorable response per condition. The individuals who were not included all had no scorable response in the passive condition. For the 17 individuals included in the analysis, there was no difference between the two conditions ($p > 0.40$ by Fisher's exact).

However, the lack of a difference between the temporal adjunct conditions should not be construed as evidence of an adultlike pattern. Four of our typically developing children showed an agent strategy in interpreting the two temporal conditions (resulting in a correct interpretation of the active temporal condition, and an incorrect construal of the object of the *by*-phrase as PRO in the passive condition), and two children showed a patient strategy (resulting in an incorrect interpretation in the active condition and a correct interpretation in the passive condition). There was no clear cut evidence in favour of either strategy in the act-out task for the individuals with Down Syndrome, although one individual showed a pattern consistent an agent strategy and another showed a pattern consistent with a patient strategy, as given in Table 3.4. In addition, one individual had a clear cut pattern of choosing the nearest NP to PRO in all (4/4) responses for each condition (incorrect for both conditions). The remaining individuals showed no discernible pattern in their responses.

3.3.3 *Written Test*

One participant did not do the written test. In this test, participants chose one of two answers to a question following a written sentence. The sentence types were again those illustrated in (1–10). Sample materials and questions for each construction are given in (1′–10′),

1′. Simple active sentences
Mom kisses Dad
Who kisses? Mom ☐ Dad ☐

2′. Simple passive sentences
Dad is kissed by Mom
Who kisses? Mom ☐ Dad ☐

3′. Complement to *tell/ask*: main clause active
Sue tells Paul to kiss Mom
Who kisses Mom? Sue ☐ Paul ☐

4′. Complement to *tell/ask*: main clause passive
Sue is told by Paul to kiss Mom
Who kisses Mom? Sue ☐ Paul ☐

5′. Complement to *promise*
Sue promises Paul to kiss Mom
Who kisses Mom? Sue ☐ Paul ☐

6′. *eager* predicates
Sue is eager to kiss
What happens? Someone kisses Sue ☐ Sue kisses someone ☐

7′. *easy* predicates
Sue is easy to kiss
What happens? Someone kisses Sue ☐ Sue kisses someone ☐

8′. Temporal adjunct clause: main clause active
Sue kisses Mom before jumping over the fence
Who jumps over the fence? Sue ☐ Mom ☐

9′. Temporal adjunct clause: main clause passive
Sue is kissed by Mom before jumping over the fence
Who jumps over the fence? Sue ☐ Mom ☐

10′. Complement to *choose* with a prepositional object gap
Sue chooses Paul to read to
What happens? Sue reads to Paul ☐ Paul reads to Sue ☐

As in the act-out task, there were a total of six tokens of sentences types (1–2) and four tokens of the remaining sentence types, presented over the three testing sessions with more challenging constructions introduced in the second and third sessions. A quarter of the materials were sentence tokens also used in the act-out, the remaining were new to the written task.[3] In half the materials the correct answer was the first answer given for the subject to choose from, in the remaining half it was the second answer. The materials were printed in 20 point type and participants were given as long as they wished to do the task. The complete set of materials is given in Appendix 2.

[3] A comparison of performance on those items that were shared in the act-out and written tests with those that were new to the written test revealed no difference in levels of success for the shared vs. new items.

3.3.4 Results of the Written Test

Figures 3.3 and 3.4 present the results in terms of percentage correct responses, with participants grouped by age equivalence on the PPVT (Fig. 3.3) and success on the simple passive in the written task (Fig. 3.4). For the written test, there were no significant correlations between any of the standardized tests, except for a negative correlation between Gates MacGinitie Grade Equivalence and performance on temporal active sentences ($r = -0.47$, $p < 0.02$). Although it might be that this correlation reflects a reliance by less able subjects on a first NP = subject of the subordinate clause strategy, which for this clause type will yield the correct result, the number of comparisons performed (footnote 2), and the fact that the correlation was significant and positive for the act-out, makes such an interpretation tenuous.

Since the written test was a forced choice test with two possible answers (corresponding to the subject and direct or prepositional object of the main clause), there were no unscorable responses for this test, with the exception of a very small number of failures to respond. None of the paired comparisons carried out for the act-out (*tell*-active vs. *tell*-passive, *tell*-active vs. *promise*, *eager* vs. *easy*) were significant by Fisher's exact. The total responses for each comparison are given in Table 3.5.

Although the comparison between *eager* and *easy* was not significant, it is plausible that the written test benefitted some individuals with DS. In this test, six persons showed perfect performance with *eager* sentences, making the main clause subject refer to the embedded clause subject. These six persons gave correct object responses to *easy* sentences between 2 and 4 times (mean 2.67). In comparison, six persons also performed perfectly in the act-out test (the groups overlapped by two persons), but their correct object responses to the *easy* sentences were lower, with five out of the six giving one object response and one giving 2 (mean 1.17). Thus the written test may have promoted more correct responses to *easy* predicates for those individuals who scored the maximum for *eager* predicates.

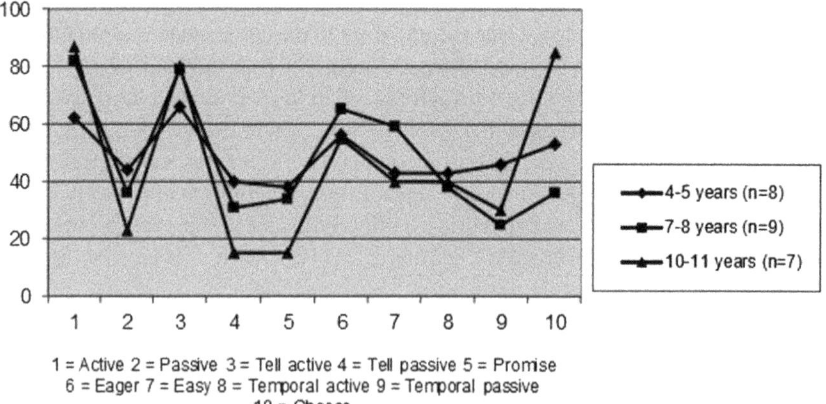

Fig. 3.3 Written test mean percentage correct: DS grouped by PPVT equivalents

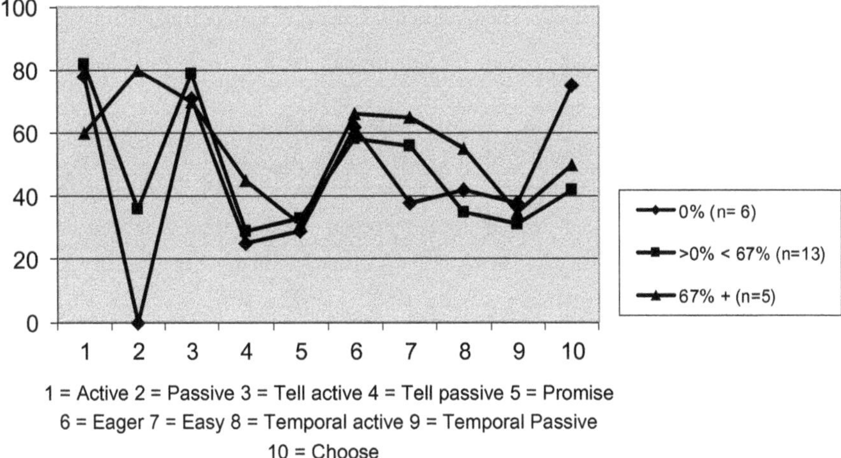

Fig. 3.4 Written test mean percentage correct: DS grouped by success on simple passive (written)

The data for temporal active vs. temporal passive produced more patterned results for the written test than for the act-out. We classified participants who had 3 or 4 responses of a given type (subject or direct/prepositional object) to both the temporal active and passive conditions. Two participants had an adult-like response pattern, making PRO refer to the subject of the main clause. The pattern of agent reference for PRO (subject response for active and object response for passive), the pattern of patient reference for PRO (object response for active and subject response for passive) were both present. The largest group of participants had a pattern of reference to the linearly closest NP (object in the temporal active condition and object of the preposition for the temporal passive condition). The number of participants in each category is given in Table 3.6.

In our data for typically developing children, we found no clear pattern of reference to the linearly closest NP for the temporal clause conditions. McDaniel et al. (1990/91) did find some 4–5 year old children who preferred to interpret both the object of the active main clause as coreferential with the PRO subject of an adjunct and sentences with the main clause verb *tell* as (correctly) coreferential with the PRO subject of an infinitival complement (a finding that is relevant to our data, see below).[4] There has never been a written test for typically developing children who were old enough to do one, and so it is not clear if the linear strategy is a function of the task used, or is a pattern used by persons with DS that is similar to that of the children in McDaniel et al's study.

[4] The study by McDaniel et al. (1990/91) did not include prepositional objects in the main clause, and it is thus unclear if they have a linear preference, or would have reacted differently with passive or locative PPs in the main clause.

Table 3.5 Written test: Distribution of responses for paired comparisons with PRO

Tell active vs. *tell* passive

	Number of responses	
	Subject	Object
Tell-A	24	72
Tell-P	30	66

Fisher's exact, p > .40

Tell active vs. *Promise*

	Number of responses	
	Subject	Object
Tell-A	24	72
Promise	30	67

Fisher's exact, p > .30

Eager vs. *Easy*

	Number of responses	
	Subject	Object
Eager	58	36
Easy	47	48

Fisher's exact, p > .10

Table 3.6 Written test: Active and passive temporal conditions response patterns

	Number of participants with pattern
Subject	2
Agent	2
Patient	1
Object	10
Unclassifiable	9

3.3.5 *Act-Out Comprehension vs. Written Comprehension: A Comparison*

We discuss three differences between the results of the act-out test and the written test: (1) the lack of any significant difference in the written test for the paired comparisons between *tell*-active vs. *tell*-passive, *tell*-active vs. *promise*, and *eager* vs. *easy* constructions (modulo the difference in performance for *eager* vs *easy* mentioned above for individuals who scored perfectly on *eager* sentences); (2) a higher performance for *tell* active sentences in the written test; and (3) the more patterned responses in the written test to the temporal active and passive conditions.

The lack of significance on the paired comparisons may be due to the forced choice test, in which there were virtually no unscorable responses. This may have introduced a randomness into the data, i.e. responses for which the participants were unsure of the correct response were scored. If such responses were distributed evenly between the paired conditions, this would have inflated the numbers for each condition and diluted the difference between conditions.

Performance on the simple passive on the act-out produced groupings that differentiated participants on condition 3 (active *tell* sentences); see Table 3.7. On the written task, average performance on this condition was high (never less than 60%), regardless of the grouping measure used.

Performance on the active *tell* sentences is high in typically developing children. We originally hypothesized that the written task might produce overall higher levels

Table 3.7 Comparison of performance on *tell* active sentences: Mean percentage correct act-out and written tests

PPVT Grouping

	Act-out	Written
4-5 years	44	65
7-8 years	68	80
10-11 years	65	80

Passive act-out Grouping

	Act-out	Written
Low	44	62
Inter	53	80
Upper	86	82

of correct responses than the act-out task, the latter requiring the participant to recall the sentence read to him or her and then perform the act-out. In the written task, the subject could study the written sentence for as long as s/he wished, and certainly many of our participants attended very closely to the materials, appearing to make considered choices rather than just ticking one answer or the other. And so it appeared possible that the written task might have given individuals with DS the opportunity to display their ability with this early-acquired piece of grammar. However, performance on simple active sentences was worse on the written test than on the act-out test (sign test, $z = 4.690$, $p < 0.00001$), contrary to what we would expect if performance was always higher on the written test for skills that are early acquired. A sign test on the number correct for act-out vs. written scores for *tell* active sentences was not significant ($z = 1.601$, $p > 0.10$), although there was a trend towards better performance in the written test. We return below to the better performance on the written test for *tell* active sentences.

The third difference between the act-out and written tests was a clearer patterning of results for the written test in the case of temporal active and passive conditions. In the act-out task, only one individual with DS showed a clear pattern of reference to the linearly nearest NP to PRO, and one participant had a pattern weakly consistent with an agent strategy and another weakly consistent with a patient strategy. In the written test, over half (15/24) showed an identifiable pattern, with three or four responses of a given type to each condition; see Table 3.6. Ten participants had a pattern of reference to the linearly nearest NP to PRO. As noted above, reference to the linearly closest NP has not clearly been observed in typically developing children, and yet it accounts for the largest group of persons with DS with a classifiable pattern in the written test.

Is it the case that reference to the linearly closest NP can account for the relative success in the written task with *tell* active sentences? Twelve individuals with DS showed a pattern of preference to the closest NP for both *tell* active and *tell* passive sentences. (No individual showed any of the other patterns identified for temporal active and passive sentences.) Thus we can account for the relative success in terms of a predilection for choosing the closest NP as referent of PRO in the written test.[5]

[5] In addition, there are two instances in the data which appear to be candidates for a case of regression towards the mean (the phenomenon whereby individuals who happen to score above their real ability on a first test do worse on a second test and individuals who happen to score below their real ability on a first test do better on a second test). First, individuals in the Upper Group on the simple passive grouping got worse in the written test on simple passive (dropping to around 40% correct) and individuals in the Lower Group improved performance on the written test (rising to around 30% correct). Second, for the *easy* construction, for both the PPVT grouping and the passive grouping, the mean correct for object gap predicates was lower for the Low and Intermediate Groups on the act-out than on the written task, and the reverse was true for the Upper Group. While we cannot rule out some regression towards the mean effect in the data, the testing sequence argues against this as a complete explanation. In each of the three testing sessions, each participant received first a portion of the act-out battery and then a portion of the written battery. Two tokens of the simple passive were included in each testing session. Five individuals in the high group whose performance got worse on the simple passive and three individuals in the low group whose performance improved each showed a pattern of contrast (poorer/better performance) between the act-out and written tasks

3.4 Discussion

3.4.1 The Passive

We have assumed that the passive of action verbs is acquired in normal development by 3 to 4 years of age, and our typically developing group confirmed this to be correct. However, there is not complete agreement on this in the literature, Miolo et al. (2005), found that typically developing children aged 3–5 scored only approximately 50% correct on the semantic role (agent vs. patient) assignment in passive sentences. In our test, we used only materials that were optimally designed to tap knowledge of the passive: the verbs were actional and took a direct object. Factors such as the use of non-action verbs and the use of *by*-phrases may depress performance in the passive (see Chap. 5). Miolo et al. included passives formed by the passivization of a prepositional object (e.g. *The white sheep is jumped over by the red cow*), which are regarded as marginal in the linguistic literature, requiring an extra operation to incorporate the preposition with the verb as a unit (Hornstein and Weinberg 1981).[6]

Of our participants, seven with DS scored 67% or more correct on the act-out test of the passive (of whom six scored perfectly). Rondal (1995) demonstrated that his subject, Françoise, perfectly comprehended the passive, with both action and non-action verbs, and with and without the *par* ('by') phrase. Rubin (2006) tested the passive with DS participants, using act-out, picture selection, repetition and interrogation ('Who *verb*ed?' Who was *verb*ed?') to test comprehension, and imitation to test production. One participant scored above chance (and on occasion 100% correct), while the remaining nine participants scored at or below chance. Overall, it is clear that some persons with DS 'get' the passive. But what can be said of those that perform at or below chance?

Bridges and Smith (1984) and Rubin (2006) take the view that chance performance shows that persons with DS are beginning to comprehend the passive. This is reasonable, to the extent that the contrast between perfect/above chance performance on active sentences needs to be accounted for. However, are persons with DS really beginning to understand the passive, or merely to recognise that something is amiss with their expectation of an active sentence? Evidence in favour of a true understanding of the passive comes from improved performance on short passives (lacking a *by*-phrase). Rubin found such evidence in the repetition task and the picture selection comprehension task, and further evidence is presented in Chap. 5. Notice also that the grouping by the performance on the simple passive produced an ordering parallel to that for typically developing children for the *eager* vs. *easy* predicates in

---

in at least two of the three testing sessions. This indicates a task-based difference in performance that does not derive from the sequence of tests. Moreover, a regression to the mean effect does not explain the consistently better performance (albeit via a non-grammatical strategy) on active *tell* sentences or the more patterned responses to temporal active and passive sentences in the written test.

[6] The children in Miolo et al.'s study did not do markedly better on active sentences. The testing situation (with a context set of animals either visible or not visible) may have depressed performance.

both the act-out and written tasks; this is consistent with a developing awareness of a gap in object position shared by the passive and the *easy* construction.

3.4.2 Orders of Acquisition in Persons with DS

Does language development in persons with DS follow the same path that it does in typically developing children? Our answer based on this study is both yes and no. The PPVT age equivalent scores are ranked in order from highest (10–11 years), intermediate (7–8) to lowest (4–5) for some of the constructions we tested, and no ranking goes clearly against this order for the remaining constructions. However, *promise*, which for typically developing children shows a clear leap from virtually zero correct to over 80% correct between 4–5 and 7–8 years, does not show a similar jump for the persons with DS. But the comparison between the *tell* active construction and *promise* is significant or near significant for the intermediate and upper groups on the act-out task, indicating that although performance is not anywhere near perfect, there is some awareness of the special control property of *promise*.

A similar point can be made with respect to *eager* vs. *easy*. Although there is a contrast between the two types of predicate in Table 3.3, an analysis of the data from individual predicates showed that no particular predicate led the way in correct responses, contrary to the results for our typical children, and the results reported in McKee (1997).

3.4.3 Comprehension Skills by Persons with DS

Although absolute levels of performance are generally quite low, our participants with DS demonstrate some knowledge of the syntax of complex sentences. Specifically, as revealed by the Fisher exact analyses in Tables 3.1–3.3, in the act-out task our subjects:

a. Use main clause syntax/thematic structure in computing the reference of the PRO subject of the complement to *tell/ask*.
b. Have some knowledge of lexical exceptions to general rules (*tell* vs. *promise*)
c. Have some knowledge of the *easy* object gap construction.

With respect to our participants' performance with temporal clauses in the act-out test, it is important to consider whether a simple first-NP-is-subject (PRO) strategy is being used when a correct response is given, rather than knowledge of the rule of interpretation based on c-command. There are solid linguistic grounds in adult grammar for the rule of interpretation. As sketched in Chap. 2, the temporal clause is attached high in the syntactic structure (outside the VP), and the PRO subject can 'see' only the main clause subject, not the main clause object (in linguistic terms, only the main clause subject c-commands PRO). The high attachment of temporal clauses and the requirement that PRO can only refer to a c-commanding NP are plausibly general constraints on linguistic structure and hence success with this construction can be viewed as evidence of sensitivity to such strictures.

As far as our evidence goes, we suspect that both a strategy-response pattern and a rule-based response pattern may be at work in the act-out data. If we restrict ourselves to just the active temporal condition (since performance was overall poor in the passive condition) and examine the whole group of 25 individuals, we find 5/7 persons in the lower group on passive performance, 2/10 in the intermediate group, and 5/8 in the upper group—i.e. only 20% of persons scoring in the intermediate group on passive, compared with 71% and 62% in the lower and upper groups, respectively. This is consistent with the use of a strategy by the low group and use of grammar by the upper group.[7]

We have found evidence of comprehension knowledge of the syntax of complex sentences in individuals with DS (embedded clauses and associated rules of PRO subject interpretation), and evidence of knowledge of the lexicon/syntax interface (lexical restrictions on syntactic constructions). But it is far from the case that our participants are performing in a completely parallel way to typically developing children, as the absence of a jump in performance from lower to intermediate level for *promise* illustrates. And we have evidence from the active and passive temporal conditions and the active and passive *tell* conditions that individuals with DS may use a linear strategy of reference to the nearest NP to the empty category PRO, a strategy that is used rarely (if ever) by typically developing children (footnote 4). Such a strategy may also account for the overall poor performance on *promise*.

This is cross-sectional data, and so it is difficult to draw conclusions about the course of learning, but the data is at least consistent with the idea that syntactic development may continue through adolescence and young adulthood for individuals with DS (a point that we return to in Chap. 4). Interestingly in this regard, we also looked at the correlation between chronological age and success on the test constructions; for *choose* in the act-out task success significantly correlated with chronological age ($r = 0.53$, $p < 0.007$) and this is the construction that is mastered latest by typically developing children

The development of syntax by young adults is supported by the results of a follow up, done 12 years after the initial testing. JT, JN and MN took part in the follow up, which repeated the act-out comprehension test in the initial battery.[8] JT and JN were amongst the highest scorers on the initial test, and MN was a moderate performer. At the first testing, their chronological ages were 33;10 (JT), 30;11 (JN) and 24;02 (MN). The results showed no significant difference between the scores on the two tests for JT and JN, but there was a significant improvement in the performance of MN. MN scored higher for 7 of the 10 constructions included in the battery on the

[7] It should be noted that the PPVT did not produce a distinction between the intermediate and the upper/lower groups, with 4/5 in the upper group, 6/12 in the intermediate group and 2/8 in the lower group, and thus the evidence for a division between use of a linear vs. grammatical analysis is equivocal.

[8] These three participants also did the picture verification test on pronouns and reflexives reported in Chap. 6.

second test than on the first test, and equally on the remaining three ($z = 2.686$, $p = < 0.009$, by sign test, 2 tail).

In addition, our data invites comparison with one aspect of the results of Fowler et al. (1994). Fowler et al. studied DS participants' use of some of the grammatical morphemes studied by Brown (1973). They found that progress was made on morphemes which are later mastered by typically developing children, even though earlier acquired morphemes had not been mastered. Similarly, our data shows progress being made with *easy* and some success with *choose*, despite the fact that performance on *promise* remains at a fairly low level.[9]

References

Bridges, A., and J. Smith. 1984. Syntactic comprehension in Down's syndrome children. *British Journal of Psychology* 75: 187–196.

Brown, R. 1973. *A first language.* Cambridge, MA: Harvard University Press.

Carrow-Woolfolk, E. 1985. *Test for auditory comprehension of language* (*TACL-R*). Ann Arbor, MI: Pro-Ed.

Dunn, D., and D. Dunn. 1997. *Peabody picture vocabulary test*, 3rd ed. Circle Pines, MN: American Guidance Service.

Fowler, A., R. Gelman, and L. Gleitman. 1994. The course of language learning in children with Down Syndrome: Longitudinal and language level comparisons with young normally developing children. In *Constraints on language acquisition: Studies of atypical children*, ed. H. Tager-Flusberg. Hillsdale, NY: Lawrence Erlbaum Associates.

Frizelle, P., P. Thompson, M. Duta, and D. Bishop. 2019. The understanding of complex syntax in children with Down Syndrome. *Wellcome Open Research* 3: 140 (34 pp.).

Hornstein, N., and A. Weinberg. 1981. Case theory and preposition stranding. *Linguistic Inquiry* 12: 55–92.

Joffe, V., and S. Varlokosta. 2007. Patterns of syntactic development in children with Williams Syndrome and Down's Syndrome: Evidence from passives and Wh-Questions. *Clinical Linguistics and Phonetics* 21: 705–727.

MacGinitie, W., and R. MacGinitie. 1989. *Gates-MacGinitie reading tests (GMRT)*, 3rd ed. Riverside Publishing.

McDaniel, D., H. Cairns, and J. Ryan Hsu. 1990/91. Control principles in the grammars of young children. *Language Acquisition* 1: 297–335.

McKee, C. 1997. Some adjectives are 'easy' and some are not. *Lexicology* 3: 59–83.

Miolo, G., R. Chapman, and H. Sindberg. 2005. Sentence comprehension in adolescents with Down Syndrome: Role of sentence voice, visual context, and auditory-verbal short term memory. *Journal of Speech, Language and Hearing Research* 48: 172–188.

Rondal, J. 1995. *Exceptional language development in Down Syndrome.* Cambridge, UK: Cambridge University Press.

Rubin, M. Coelho de Barros Pereira. 2006. The passive in adolescents with Down Syndrome: A case study. *Down Syndrome Research and Practice* 11: 88–96.

[9] A recent study by Frizelle et al. (2019) reports low performance on the comprehension of complex syntax by children with Down Syndrome, using different constructions (although complements to V were used, the verbs were different, and the adverbial clauses in their study were tensed). The individuals with Down Syndrome in that study were considerably younger than those in this study and those in Thordardottir et al. (2002, see Chap. 4), with an age range of 6;10 to 11;08, and (as Frizelle et al. point out) they may yet develop as they grow older.

Thordardottir, E., R. Chapman, and L. Wagner. 2002. Complex syntax production by adolescents with Down Syndrome. *Applied Psycholinguistics* 23: 163–183.

Wechsler, D. 1991. *Wechsler Intelligence Scale for Children*, 3rd ed. Toronto, ON: Harcourt Assessment.

Chapter 4
Production Data

Abstract A speech sample was elicited from the participants with Down Syndrome (DS) who took part in the comprehension tests reported in Chap. 3, with the aid of a wordless picture book. The participants produced a range of complex syntactic structures, the most frequent being conjoined sentences, post-posed reason/purpose clauses and infinitival complements to V. Lexical variation was found for many of the structures (for example, infinitival complements to V occurred with seven different main verbs). The range of structures produced developed with the age of the participants, with the oldest group (over 25 years) producing a total of 13 different structures. We make a comparison between two individuals whose scores on standardized tests were similar, but whose behaviour in the production task was notably dissimilar in terms of number of complex structures produced, cohesiveness and length of narrative.

Keywords Elicited production · Range of structures · Lexical variation · Individual variation

4.1 The Task

We elicited a speech sample from our DS participants using a wordless picture book (M. Mayer, *A boy, a dog and a frog*).[1] The sequence of pictures tells a story, the gist of which is as follows: A boy goes fishing with his dog. They get to a pond and the boy attempts to catch a frog in his net. The frog eludes the boy, who trips on a branch and falls in the water, ending up with his bucket on his head. The boy goes home with the dog. The frog, who initially was cross with the boy, begins to miss him and follows the boy's footprints to the boy's house. There he finds the boy and the dog taking a bath. He hops onto the dog's head and at the end they are (in the words of two of our participants) "one big happy family" and "actually clean and happy together".

[1] In two cases, a different story from the same series of books was used.

H. Goodluck, *Complex Syntax in the Language of Persons with Down Syndrome*, SpringerBriefs in Linguistics,
https://doi.org/10.1007/978-3-030-96440-5_4

Three of our participants did not take part in the production task, due to scheduling and other problems.

4.2 Types of Complex Syntax Produced

The goal of this analysis was to assess the range of complex structures produced by our subjects.

4.2.1 Range of Structures

The participants produced one or more of the following complex sentence types and each of these sentence types was produced by at least two subjects (examples from our data). The examples are given in regular English spelling, although the pronunciation of many of the subjects deviated from the pronunciation of the dialect of English the subjects were exposed to/spoke.

1. Conjoined clause with *and* or *but*

   Examples: So he followed the frog and went in his house (AL)
   He has the dog in the net but the frog didn't go (AV)

2. Adjunct clause of time, with *when, while, before* or *after*

   Examples: and when the boy saw the frog at the pond… (MT)
   Then when they looked it was flooded (JH)
   The most help he could give to the frog before he ran off for breakfast (JH)

3. Adjunct clause of reason or purpose, with *because*, *so* (*that*) or (*in order*) *to*

   Examples: …because she don't see the frog fall down (YI)
   …because the boy and the dog going away (PO)
   ...so the boy went after and saved him (JH)
   Here comes the dog to save the poor frog (AV)

4. Infinitival complement to V, with *to*

   Examples: …trying to get a frog (SB)
   ...did not want to play (JP)
   the boy decides to attack the frog (AL)
   ...but he forgot to shut the door (AV)

5. Gerundial complement to V

   Examples: …saw they falling down (PO)
   …saw a frog standing there (MR)
   …watching the boy having fun (RH)

6. Tensed complement to V, with *that* or without *that*

   Examples: …it appears that the boy is fishing with his pet dog (JN)
   …the dog had noticed that the frog was just playing dead (MN)
   He said maybe he's singing "Stella ella olga" (RH)
   They found out the frog was drowning (JH)

7. *Yes–no/Wh-* complement to V

   Examples: I don't know why he's doing it (RH)
   I don't know what the heck is he doing there (RH)
   He doesn't know if it's a frog or not (RH)
   …want to see if it catch it (SB)

8. Headed relative clause (with *wh-W*ord, *that* or zero)

   Examples: I see a boy who is climbing on a tree (RH)
   …his pet dog who fell asleep (JN)
   …the tree that had a hole in there (MT)
   …a happy boy that is going down to catch some fish (JT)

9. Free relative

   Examples: …didn't get what he wanted (MT)
   …I don't know whatever's going to happen (RH)

10. Infinitival complement to *eager*-type Adjective (subject gap)

    Examples: …She afraid to fall down (YI)
    happy… to see him again (JH)
    He's so excited to see the frog again (AV)

11. Tensed complement to Adjective

    Examples: He was afraid they catch him (MR)
    ...angry that the frog has to go on (JT)

12. Direct quote

    Examples: He say 'go away' (PO)
    The boy said 'not you again' (JH)

In addition to the complex sentence types above, there were also a number of constructions that occurred only once in the data and/or were used only by one subject, which we list here:

13. Infinitival relative clause

    He doesn't have no friends left to play with (RH)

14. Complement to *easy*-type adjective (Object Gap)

    He's too far away to catch (AV)

15. Comparative clause

...and the frog was laughing like he was taking LSD (MT)
...dog was jumping and skipping like he was going cuckoo (MT)

4.3 Coding Decisions

We adopted the following rules for inclusion/exclusion in the data set.

Included

i. All subjects' utterances that were clauses that directly/spontaneously described the pictures.
ii. Utterances that were responses to the experimenter's prompts, provided they addressed the content of the story.
iii. Utterances that contained no verb, where the copula could be inserted in the place of the missing verb.
iv. Utterances that contained unintelligible item(s), provided the unintelligible item could be replaced with a single word.

Excluded

i. Utterances that were commentary/conversation with the experimenter and/or other persons present (the videographer, observer and/or parent or relative).
ii. Utterances that were of dubious/ambiguous grammatical structure.

These rules were in practice not always easy to follow, particularly in the case of dubious/ambiguous items, and a degree of judgement was sometimes exercised. For example, in the grammar of English a standard diagnostic for a *wh*-clause being analysed as a free relative rather than a *wh*-complement to a verb is whether the *wh*-word can be replaced by the form *wh-ever.* We applied this diagnostic in categorising RH's utterance in (9) above as a free relative, but of course we can't know for sure that RH's grammar included this component of the grammar of free relatives. Another example is the use of *when* by one of our subjects (MT). He produced many *when* (and *while*) clauses in isolation, suggesting that he was using *when* to mean (*and*) *then.* We decided accordingly not to code these as adjunct clauses. However, we did not wish to make a rule that any potential adjunct clauses that were not accompanied by a main clause should be excluded, since some of our subjects produced such 'lone' adjuncts in contexts that suggested that they were not main clauses (for example, in response to the experimenter's prompts or as a continuation of a previous utterance).

Table 4.1 Distribution of conjunctions

Lexical item	Frequency	Number of participants contributing
and	64	20
but	8	5
Total	72	20[a]

[a]The total number of participants contributing in this and subsequent tables is less than the total derived by adding the numbers in the column above the total, since some individuals contributed to more than one row

Table 4.2 Distribution of reason/purpose adjuncts

Lexical item	Frequency	Number of participants contributing
Post-posed		
(be)cause	29	8
(in order) to	9	6
in order to	1	1
so	8	5
that	1	1
Total	48	18

4.4 Frequency and Lexical Breakdown of Complex Sentence Types Produced

The following Sects. (4.4.1–4.4.6) give breakdowns of the frequency of usage of the different constructions listed above, and the lexical items they were associated with. The reader may at this point wish to consult Sect. 4.4.7 for a less detailed analysis.

4.4.1 Conjunctions

All but three subjects produced one or more conjoined clauses. Table 4.1 gives the distribution of different forms of conjunction.[2]

4.4.2 Adjuncts

Tables 4.2 and 4.3 give the breakdown in use of reason/purpose and temporal adjuncts, in post-posed and pre-posed position. Where an adjunct was produced without a main clause, in response to an experimenter prompt/question, it was coded as post-posed.

[2] There were also instances of juxtaposition of sentences, which we have not included in the table. Since all but one of the participants produced conjoined sentences with *and* and *but* in addition to the use of juxtaposition, minimal distortion of the data results from the omission of such utterances.

Table 4.3 Distribution of temporal adjuncts

Lexical item	Frequency	Number of participants contributing
A. Pre-posed		
when	4	2
while	4	3
before	1	1
after	1	1
Total	10	6
B. Post-posed		
when	5	5
while	8	3
before	1	1
as	1	1
Total	15	8

4.4.3 Complements to V

Table 4.4 gives the distribution of infinitival complements and gerundial complements to V.
Table 4.5 gives the distribution of tensed complements to V.
Table 4.6 gives the distribution of interrogative complements to V.

4.4.4 Complement to A(djective)

Tables 4.7 and 4.8 give the distribution of infinitival and tensed complements to adjectives.

4.4.5 Relative Clauses

Tables 4.9 and 4.10 give the distribution of tensed and free relative clauses, respectively.

Table 4.4 Distribution of non-finite complements to V

Main verb	Frequency	Number of participants contributing
A. Infinitival complements		
want to	11	7
decide to	7	3
try to	11	5
have to	3	2
be better to	1	1
ask NP *to*	1	1
tell NP *to*	2	1
Total	36	16
B. Gerundial complements		
see NP V-*ing*	1	1
notice NP V-*ing*	1	1
find NP V-*ing*	1	1
watch NP V-*ing*	1	1
end up V-*ing*	2	1
keep V-*ing*	1	1
Total	7	5

Table 4.5 Distribution of tensed complements to V

Main verb	Frequency		Number of participants contributing
	+*that*	−*that*	
realise	1	–	1
appear	1	–	1
learn	1	–	1
notice	2	–	1
mean	1	–	1
find out	1	1	2
think	–	1	1
Total	7	2	5

Table 4.6 Distribution of interrogative complements to V

Main verb	Frequency	Number of participants contributing
know what	3	2
know who	1	1
know how	1	1
know if	1	1
see if	1	1
Total	7	3

Table 4.7 Distribution of infinitival complements to A(djective)

Adjective	Frequency	Number of participants contributing
happy to	3	3
excited to	1	1
shocked to	1	1
afraid to	1	1
scared to	1	1
Total	7	4

Table 4.8 Distribution of tensed complements to A(djective)

Adjective	Frequency		Number of participants contributing
	+*that*	−*that*	
happy	5	–	2
surprised	1	–	1
grumpy and nasty	1	–	1
angry	–	1	1
sad	–	1	1
Total	7	2	2

Table 4.9 Distribution of tensed relative clauses

Position relativised	Frequency			Number of participants contributing
Pronoun/complementiser	+*wh*	+*that*	zero	
Subject	9	2	–	6
Direct object	–	–	1	1
Prepositional object	1	–	–	1
Total	10	2	1	6

Table 4.10 Distribution of free relative clauses

Position relativized	Frequency		Number of participants contributing
	who(ever)	*what*	
Subject	2	1	2
Direct object	–	5	3
Total	2	6	5

4.4.6 *Direct Quotation*

Direct quotes were almost exclusively produced following the verb *say* (the one exception followed the verb *shout*). There was a total of 16 direct quotes, with eight subjects contributing.

4.4.7 *Summary of the Types of Complex Syntax Produced*

Table 4.11 lists the number of tokens of each complex sentence type in (1–12) in order of frequency, together with the number of participants contributing to the total. As can be seen from the table, the three most frequently produced complex structures were conjunctions, post-posed reason adjuncts and infinitival complements to V, in that order. For each of these three constructions, a majority of the participants contributed to the total number produced. Next in frequency were post-posed temporal adjuncts, tensed relative clauses and pre-posed temporal adjuncts, each with 10 or more instances but with less than a majority of subjects contributing.

Table 4.11 Number of tokens of each structure

Structure	Total number	Number of participants contributing
Conjunctions	72	20
Postposed reason/purpose adjunct	48	18
Infinitival complement to V	36	16
Direct quote	16	8
Postposed temporal adjunct	15	8
Tensed relative clause	13	6
Preposed temporal adjunct	10	6
Tensed complement to V	9	5
Tensed complement to A	9	2
Free relative	8	5
Gerundial complement to V	7	5
Infinitival complement to A	7	4
Interrogative complement to V	7	3

The remaining constructions listed occur with less frequency and with fewer participants contributing, and may in some instances represent 'favourite' constructions; for example, the nine instances of tensed complements to adjectives were produced by two participants only. It is important to note in this case, as for the other constructions listed, that such utterances were not routines/memorised phrases, as evidenced by the range of lexical items involved. Moreover, the rarity of some constructions says nothing one way or the other about their presence in the grammar of individuals who did not produce them, given, amongst other things, the fact that the task did not target particular constructions.

4.5 Productivity and the Relation Between Comprehension and Production

Although the production task did not target particular constructions, there is some use of the syntactic forms we tested in our comprehension battery: Table 4.4 shows three instances of an object control verb (*tell* and *ask*); Table 4.7 shows seven instances of *eager*-type adjectives; and there was one occurrence of an *easy*-type adjective complement (example 14 above). One subject (JN) produced the full passive. We counted the number of different complex construction types (not tokens) listed in (1–12) that each subject produced, and calculated the mean number of construction types produced according to the groupings by PPVT and success on the passive that we used in analysing the data from the act-out comprehension battery. The result is given in Table 4.12. As an inspection of the numbers in Table 4.12 suggests, degree of success on the passive did not correspond to a greater number of construction types produced, whereas age equivalence on the PPVT did. The correlation between number of structures produced by each participant and percentage correct on comprehension of the passive is not significant ($r = 0.05$, $p > 0.824$); the correlation between number of structures produced and PPVT age equivalence is significant ($r = 0.62$, $p < 0.003$, two tail), as is also the correlation between chronical age and structures produced ($r = 0.56$, $p < 0.007$, two tail).

Table 4.12 Mean number of complex sentence types produced by performance on the act-out passive and PPVT

Passive	Group 1 (n = 6)	Group 2 (n = 10)	Group 3 (n = 6)
	4.67	5.30	5.33
PPVT	Group 1 (n = 7)	Group 2 (n = 10)	Group 3 (n = 5)
	3.57	5.20	7.80

Table 4.13 Age and average number of complex sentence types produced

Age groups (years)	8–11	12–16	17–20	21–4	25 +
N	3	4	8	2	5
Complex types	3.67	2.75	4.50	8.00	8.00

4.6 Comparison with Previous Studies of Syntactic Production by Individuals with DS

In this section we compare our data to the results of two studies of syntactic production by persons with DS: Chapman et al. (1998) and Thordardottir et al. (2002). Both examine material from a corpus collected by Chapman and her colleagues, analysing the data from 47 persons with DS in the 1998 study and 24 in the 2002 study. The data from these studies was (in the case of Chapman et al.) a conversational sample and (in both studies) a narrative sample. The narratives were elicited by asking subjects to tell/describe favourite stories and events, and to describe pictures of complex events. The Chapman et al. study used, *inter alia*, Mean Length of Utterance (MLU) as a means of comparing their DS subjects with typically developing control subjects; the MLU levels produced for the DS subjects were 2.45 (conversation) and 3.00 (narrative) and for the controls were 4.02 (conversation) and 4.69 (narrative). The Thordardottir et al. study employed qualitative and quantitative analysis of the syntactic structures produced, following the coding system of Paul (1981).[3]

Both the Chapman et al. and the Thordardottir et al. studies indicate that narrative data is more revealing of syntactic ability than conversational data, which may account for the fact that these studies showed greater syntactic skills than some previous work that relied on conversational samples (e.g. Fowler et al. 1994).

Table 4.13 summarises the age and mean number of complex syntactic structures produced in our study, using the four year age groupings employed by Chapman et al., with two additional groups for the older participants in our study. The table indicates a progression through the two lowest, middle, and two highest age groups in number of complex structures produced. As noted above, both PPVT age equivalence and chronological age correlated positively with the number of structures produced by each participant.

Table 4.14 gives the number of participants in each age group who produced a particular complex sentence type. This table reveals that age of the participants who produced a complex sentence type rises, culminating in at least one of the oldest participants producing all of the structures listed. In addition, the complex

[3] Paul's system is less fine grained than ours, treating conjunctions and adverbial clauses as a single category. Since these constructions have different syntactic properties and occur with different frequencies in the data, we have separated them. Our coding also includes structures not listed in the Paul system, specifically complements to adjectives.

Like Thordardottir et al. we did not treat items such as *wanna* and *gotta* as infinitives. However, this might not be a correct decision. One participant repeated the experimenter's utterance of *wanna* as *want to,* indicating that she had a mental representation of the infinitive form linked to *wanna.*

Table 4.14 Number of participants using complex constructions

Age groups (years)	8–11	12–16	17–20	21–24	25 +
N	3	4	8	2	5
Conjunction	2	3	8	2	5
Postposed reason	3	2	6	2	5
Infinitival complement to V	1	3	6	2	5
Direct quote	1	2	2	0	3
Postposed temporal	2	1	2	2	2
Tensed relative	0	0	1	2	3
Preposed temporal	1	1	1	2	1
Tensed complement to A	0	0	0	1	2
Tensed complement to V	0	2	0	1	5
Free relative	0	0	1	0	4
Gerundial complement to V	0	0	1	2	3
Infinitival complement to A	1	0	2	0	2
Interrogative complement to V	0	0	2	0	1
Total number of constructions used	7	7	11	9	13
Percentage of constructions used	54	54	84	69	100

sentence types that were produced only once or by only one participant (13–15) were contributed by one participant in the 17 to 20 age group (who contributed 14), and two in the 25+ age group (who contributed 13 and 15).

4.7 A Comparison of Two Individuals

Our data contains one striking contrast between two subjects, JT and MT, on the comprehension and production tasks. These two subjects have scores that are not too dissimilar on standardized tests, as shown in Table 4.15.

Table 4.15 Standardized test scores, JT and MT

	PPVT[a]	TACL[b] Word	TACL Grammatical	TACL Elaborated	Gates-MacGinitie[c]
JT	10;03	87.5	50	47.5	3.4
MT	9;11	95	47.5	35	2.2

[a]Age equivalent scores
[b]Percentage correct
[c]Grade equivalent score

However, JT clearly outperforms MT on the comprehension tasks. For example, in the first battery of act-out tests, MT shows evidence that he relies to some degree on a 'first N = agent' strategy, leading him to correctly interpret the PRO subject of the complement to *promise* (*Mom promises Dad* PRO *to leave*), but to make errors with the PRO subject of the complement to *tell* (*Mom tells Dad* PRO *to leave*). In the first act-out battery, MT scored only 2/6 correct on the simple passive, whereas JT scored 6/6 correct. In the passive experiments reported in the next chapter, MT is one of three subjects characterised as having global problems with the passive, whereas JT is one of the subjects who show a pattern of difficulty with experiencer passives when a *by*-phrase is present (*Mom was heard by Dad*).

Despite the fact that MT is clearly not as competent as JT in the comprehension tasks, their performance on the elicited production task does not completely fit with this difference in ability. JT conveyed the gist of the story, in approximately 160 words. She produced four types of embedded clauses (a reduced *in order to* clause, an infinitival complement to the verb *try*, a tensed complement to the verb *think*, and a free relative clause) and she also produced a full passive (with the *by* phrase). MT produced almost 1000 words, with only a moderately coherent story line, but with a fairly fluent delivery and a syntactically diverse range of sentences. These comprised: pre-posed temporal adjunct clauses; post-posed temporal and reason clauses; infinitival complements to the verbs *decide* and *want*; gerundial complements to the verbs *watch* and *find*; a tensed complement to the verb *realise*; a direct quote following the verb *say*; a tensed relative clause with a subject gap introduced by *that*; a relative with the wh-word and *be* deleted (*...everything hanging in front of him*); free relative clauses; and tensed comparative clauses (e.g. *...like he was going cuckoo*).

The performance of MT on the production task thus indicates that comprehension ability may not always be indicative of the range of complex syntax that an individual with DS has at his/her disposal.

4.8 Other Observations

4.8.1 Command of the Article System

We observed an imperfect command of the article system in several subjects, reflected primarily in a failure to switch from *a* to *the* after first mention of an entity. Examples are given in (16) and (17),

16. OK there is a dog and a boy is going fishing and he has a bucket and a net and a dog snooping around. And a boy saw a [unintelligible] frog... (SS)
17. a boy ... a dog look at trees, a boy fishing [unintelligible] the water ... a boy hold on, get fish up. Oh my god, a dog hanging down ... (K-A W).

This suggests that while it is commonly observed that persons with DS have relatively good pragmatic and conversational skills—in the sense, for example, of appropriate turn taking—these skills may not always extend to the linguistic means of structuring a discourse. Other individuals, however, did appropriately use the definite and indefinite articles.

4.8.2 *Creativity*

Some participants also provided examples of their command of grammar in terms of creative use of morphological rules when they did not know an appropriate word or could not immediately access one. Examples are given in (18–20),

18. Experimenter: What's going on here?
    YJ: A frog [unintelligible] s- stepprints.
    Experimenter: What are these?
    YJ: s- s- stepprint

(YJ subsequently learns the word *footprint* from the experimenter and uses it a few turns later, although he subsequently reverts to *stepprint.*)

19. …and the dog said goodbye and all of a sudden he looked at him in a sad puppy-looking face (RH, describing the frog).
20. …the frog had a bad day but he decided to go on the leaf and did pond surfing (MT).

4.9 Discussion

The analysis of production data in this chapter complements the comprehension data presented in Chap. 3. First, it gives us a fuller picture of the range of syntactic constructions within the grasp of our participants. Second, the range of lexical items used in the various structures provides evidence that the use of complex syntax is not limited to routines and/or particular words.

In addition, it feeds into a debate concerning a critical age for language development in persons with DS. The limited development of complex syntax has been documented in many studies (including Fowler et al. 1994; Rondal 1996 [cited in Thordardottir et al. 2002], and Chapman et al. 1998), and has led to the claim that persons with DS may pass an age at which complex syntax can be attained—in effect, their language reaches a plateau before syntactic complexity is reached (see Fowler et al. 1994). Thordardottir et al. (2002) challenge this proposal, by showing that their participants (who were aged up to 20 years) did use complex syntax. Our data supplements this finding, by showing that the use of complex syntax increases both quantitatively (Table 4.13) and qualitatively (Table 4.14) with age, and continues into the oldest age group (more than 25 years). Whether or not this can be attributed to the fact that our participants could read is not a question that this study can answer. However, it suggests that age per se is not the critical factor, but rather exposure to language at a certain point. A comparison with studies of deaf individuals is pertinent. Newport (1990) demonstrated that deaf persons who were exposed to sign language before age six displayed a native-like competence in that language, whereas exposure after age six led to greater or lesser deficits in their knowledge.

References

Chapman, R., H. Seung, S. Schwartz, and E. Kay-Raining Bird. 1998. Language skills of children and adolescents with Down syndrome: II. Production deficits. *Journal of Speech, Language and Hearing Research* 41: 861–873.

Fowler, A., R. Gelman, and L. Gleitman. 1994. The course of language learning in children with Down Syndrome: Longitudinal and language level comparisons with young normally developing children. In *Constraints on language acquisition: Studies of atypical children*, ed. H. Tager-Flusberg. Hillsdale, NY: Lawrence Erlbaum Associates.

Mayer, M. 1978. *A boy, a dog and a frog*. New York: Dial Books for Young Readers, Pied-Piper Printing edition.

Newport, E. 1990. Maturational constraints on language learning. *Cognitive Science* 14: 11–28.

Paul, R. 1981. Analyzing complex sentence development. In *Assessing language production in children: Experimental procedures*, ed. J. Miller. Austin, TX: Pro-Ed.

Rondal, J. 1996. Oral language in Down's syndrome. In *Down's syndrome: Psychological, psychobiological and socio-cultural perspectives*, ed. J. Rondal, J. Perera, L. Nadel, and A. Comblain. San Diego, CA: Singular.

Thordardottir, E., R. Chapman, and L. Wagner. 2002. Complex syntax production by adolescents with Down Syndrome. *Applied Psycholinguistics* 23: 163–183.

Chapter 5
Follow-Up Comprehension Tests

This chapter is a revised version of Eriks-Brophy et al. (2003).

Abstract Ten of the participants with Down Syndrome (DS) whose results were reported in the previous chapters took part in additional experiments. The first two experiments tested knowledge of the passive. Typically developing children have been found to do better with verbs that take the role of agent as subject (such as *kiss*) than with verbs for which the subject has the role of experiencer (such as *hear*) when a passive *by* phrase is present. However, when the *by* phrase is absent the difference between the two types of verb is reduced or eliminated. We tested the participants with DS with an act-out test and a sentence judgement test. Only two participants in the act-out test showed an amelioration for experiencer verbs when the *by*-phrase was absent, but in the sentence judgement test nine of the ten participants showed an improvement. A third experiment tested knowledge of the block on questioning from within an adverbial clause, using an (un)ambiguous question response technique. Our participants with DS, like adults and typically developing children, avoided making the question refer to a position inside an adverbial clause. Based on cross-linguistic evidence of a language that permits questions from within an adverbial clause, we argue that this is an effect of sentence processing, not an effect of the grammar of English.

Keywords Passive · *By*-phrase · Questions · Adverbial clause

5.1 Tests of the Passive and Question Formation: Participants

Ten of the participants with DS took part in three follow-up experiments. They were selected on the basis of availability and having at least one correct response out of six correct on the simple passive in the initial act-out battery. Five participants had 100% (6/6) correct on the initial battery, one had 67% (4/6), two had 33% (2/6) and two had 17% (1/6) correct. Their chronological ages ranged from 11 to 33 years. A

H. Goodluck, *Complex Syntax in the Language of Persons with Down Syndrome*, SpringerBriefs in Linguistics,
https://doi.org/10.1007/978-3-030-96440-5_5

group of 10 four to five year old typically developing children was also tested on the passive tests.

5.2 Passive Experiments

A recurrent finding in the literature on knowledge of the passive in typically developing children is that children have less difficulty with the passive of action verbs such as that in (1b), in which the subject in the active has the role of agent, than they do with the passive of verbs in which the subject in the active has the role of experiencer (2b) (e.g. Maratsos et al. 1985). In our comprehension battery (Chap. 2) we used only action verbs to test the passive.

1a Sue kisses Paul
1b Paul is kissed by Sue
2a Sue hears Paul
2b Paul is heard by Sue

Fox and Grodzinsky (1998) demonstrated that the difficulty of non-actional passives was eliminated for some children aged 3 to 5 when the *by*-phrase was removed. They suggest that this is because children have difficulty with the *by*-phrase as transmitter of a non-agentive semantic role (experiencer). On their account, children's problems are thus not with movement of the object to subject position per se, but with the semantic role transmission.

We carried out two tests of the constructions in (3),

3a Active, actional:
Paul tickled Sue
3b Active, non-actional:
Mom heard Dad in the kitchen
3c Passive, actional, + *by*-phrase:
Sue was tickled by Paul
3d Passive, non-actional, + *by*-phrase:
Dad was heard by Mom
3e Passive, non-actional, – *by*-phrase:
Dad was heard in the kitchen

The first test was an act-out task, in which subjects acted out sentences with a toy family and props. The second test was a truth value judgement task, modelled on Fox and Grodzinsky (1998). In this test, subjects judged sentences as 'true'/'right' or 'false'/'wrong' following a short (3–4 sentence) story read and acted out for them by the experimenter. Examples are given in (4) and (5).

4. Example Story for an Actional Verb
Paul tells Sue all the time about being a cry baby. Sue wants to show Paul how she is a big girl. He tells her "I will make you cry". Then he starts to tickle her. He doesn't stop until the tears run down her cheeks.
Sentence for judgement: Paul tickled Sue (Match - > True).

Table 5.1 Down syndrome participants: Mean percentage correct responses passive experiments

	Act-out	Judgment
Active, actional	98	87
Active, non-actional	82	65
Passive, actional, + by-phrase	62	52
Passive, non-actional, + by-phrase	47	42
Passive, non-actional, – by-phrase	52	75

5. Example Story for a Non-Actional Verb
   Mom has decided that no one in the house will drink pop. One night, Dad sneaks out of the bedroom to get some pop. By mistake, he drops the bottle on the floor. Mom hears Dad making noise and wakes up. Dad is cleaning up the mess when Mom walks into the room.
   Sentence for judgement: Mom was heard by Dad (Mismatch - > False).

In both tasks, each subject received four tokens of each construction tested. The test sentences were in the present tense for the act-out materials and in the past tense for the truth value judgement materials. In the sentence judgement task the correct answer was 'false' for two tokens of each construction (mismatch tokens) and 'true' for the other two tokens (match tokens). The mismatch was achieved by making the NP that is object of the verb in the story the surface subject in the test sentence (see the non-actional example 5, above). Two questionnaires were constructed, such that an item for which the correct answer was 'true' in one questionnaire had 'false' as the correct answer in the other, and vice versa. The complete set of materials is given in Appendix 3A.

The results are presented in Table 5.1, in terms of the mean percentage correct for each condition for each task.

As can be seen from Table 5.1, there was a non-trivial rise in correct responses for the experiencer passive condition without the *by*-phrase only in the case of the judgement task. We examined the performance of individual participants. The results for the act-out are given in Table 5.2. One subject scored 100% correct. There are two participants who show the Fox-Grodzinsky effect in the act-out, two who show no Fox-Grodzinsky effect and three who have global difficulty with the passive (zero or one correct response out of four for each of the three passive conditions). Table 5.3 gives the individual response patterns on the judgement task, with participants grouped according to their performance on the act-out. It can be seen from Table 5.3 that nine out of ten participants showed the Fox-Grodzinsky effect in the sense of having more correct answers to non-actional passives without *by* than non-actional passive with *by*. The difference between these conditions is significant by sign test ($z = 3$, $p < 0.003$, two tail).

Table 5.2 Down syndrome participants individual response patterns (number correct out of 4): Act-out passive experiment

Participant	Active actional	Active non-actional	Passive actional + by	Passive non-actional + by	Passive non-actional – by	Total correct
All correct						
TP	4	4	4	4	4	20
Fox-Grodzinsky pattern						
MN	4	4	3	3	4	18
JT	4	4	3	2	4	17
Mixed pattern/No Fox-Grodzinsky effect						
NF	4	4	4	3	3	18
JN	4	2	4	4	3	17
JH	4	4	2	3	3	16
AV	4	3	3	0	0	10
Global problems with passive						
JF	4	3	1	0	0	8
KW	3	3	1	0	0	7
MT	4	2	0	0	0	6

Table 5.3 Down syndrome participants individual response patterns (number correct out of four): Passive judgment experiment grouped by performance on the act-out experiment

Participant	Active actional	Active non-actional	Passive actional + by	Passive non-actional + by	Passive non-actional – by	Total correct
All correct						
TP	4	2	4	3	4	17
Fox-Grodzinsky pattern						
JT	3	3	1	2	3	12
MN	3	2	2	1	3	11
Mixed pattern/No Fox-Grodzinsky effect						
JN	3	4	3	2	4	16
NF	4	3	2	2	3	14
JH	4	3	2	2	2	13
AV	3	2	2	1	2	10
Global problems with passive						
KW	3	3	2	1	3	12
MT	4	3	2	1	2	12
JF	4	2	1	0	3	10

Table 5.4 Typically developing children: Mean percentage correct responses Passive experiments

	Act-out	Judgment
Active, actional	92	70
Active, non-actional	70	72
Passive, actional + by-phrase	95	65
Passive, non-actional, + by-phrase	57	68
Passive, non-actional − by-phrase	70	68

The performance of the 10 typically developing children we tested is given in Table 5.4. The individual response patterns of the children are given in Tables 5.5 and 5.6, using the same groupings as we used to classify the subjects with Down Syndrome. None of the children had global problems with the passive by the criterion of no more than one correct response per passive condition, although the last child in Table 5.5 came close. Table 5.5 shows that five of the children had a Fox-Grodzinsky pattern of responses, three showed no difference between the conditions, and two had the opposite pattern to that predicted. Table 5.6 shows that the largest group of children (six children) showed no difference between the conditions, two showed the Fox-Grodzinsky pattern, and two showed the opposite pattern.

Table 5.5 Typically developing children individual response patterns (number correct out of 4): Act-out passive experiment

Participant	Active actional	Active non-actional	Passive actional + by	Passive non-actional + by	Passive non-actional − by	Total correct
Fox-Grodzinsky pattern						
MB	4	4	4	3	4	19
M	4	4	3	2	4	17
TG	4	4	1	1	4	14
PW	4	4	2	1	3	14
NG	4	3	3	0	1	11
Mixed pattern/No Fox Grodzinsky effect						
VS	4	4	3	2/2	3	16/19
CB	3	4	4	3	2	16
MB	4	3	2	4	3	16
ZB	3	4	2	2	2	13
LM	3	2	2	0	0	7

Table 5.6 Typically developing children individual response patterns (number correct out of 4): judgment passive experiment grouped by performance on the act-out experiment

Participant	Active actional	Active non-actional	Passive actional + by	Passive non-actional + by	Passive non-actional − by	Total correct
Fox-Grodzinsky pattern						
MB1	4	3	4	3	3	17
M	3	3	4	3	4	17
TG	2	3	3	3	3	14
NG	3	1	3	3	3	13
PW	3	4	1	0	3	11
Mixed pattern/No Fox-Grodzinsky effect						
VS	2	3	4	4	2	15
CB	3	3	3	4	2	15
MB2	4	2	3	2	2	13
LM	2	2	2	3	3	12
ZB	2	2	2	2	2	10

5.2.1 Discussion

These experiments with the passive provide further evidence of the similarity between the behaviour of our participants with DS and typically developing children, in that the judgement experiment for individuals with DS shows clearly the contrast between experiencer passives with and without *by* that Fox and Grodzinsky observed for typically developing children.

Some comment is in order concerning the performance of our typically developing participants, in that we did not replicate the findings of Fox and Grodzinsky in our judgement task. The materials for their experiment are not published in the article by Fox and Grodzinsky, and so we cannot judge whether there was a flaw in our experimental materials, or in theirs, or an effect of a relatively small sample of children in both studies.

With the exception of a version of truth value judgement used by Perovic (2006), the truth value judgement task has not previously been used with individuals with DS, and this study thus adds to the repertoire of experimental procedures that can be used to assess language in the DS population.[1]

[1] In addition to the passive act-out test described above, participants responded to two sentence types with complements to verbs such as *choose*. The initial comprehension battery contained complements with a prepositional object gap (sentence type 10 in Chap. 2),

i. Sue chooses Paul to sing to.

5.3 Experiment on Knowledge of the Block on Questioning from within an Adjunct Clause

In the comprehension tests reported in Chap. 3, we did not test comprehension of questions, but some participants used embedded questions in their production data. We attempted a follow-up test of knowledge of the syntax of question formation in English.

5.3.1 Experiment

English is a language in which questions are formed by moving a question word to sentence-initial position (to the Complementizer Phrase). Such movement is subject to syntactic restrictions. Movement can take place from a subordinate clause that is complement to a verb, but is blocked from within an adjunct clause. This is illustrated by the contrast between (6a) and (6b),

6a Who did Sue ask Bill to meet?
6b *Who did Sue ask Bill before he met?
(cf. Sue asked Bill before he met Mary).

We gave our subjects an experiment used byGoodluck et al. (1992) to test typically developing children's knowledge of the block on questioning from within an adjunct clause. The task was (un)ambiguous question response: Subjects listened to a short (two to three sentence) story accompanied by pictures and then answered a question in which the question word could potentially refer to either the object position of

---

This is the most challenging of our test constructions for typically developing children, requiring the main clause subject to be made subject of the subordinate clause and the main clause object to be made object of the preposition (Sue sings to Paul in the example), and it is often not mastered until age 10 or older. We saw that in the initial act-out, the *choose* object gap construction was also one of the most challenging for our participants with DS. In the follow up, we compared success on the object gap *choose* construction with the same verbs without a prepositional object gap, that is, sentences such as (ii),

ii. Sue chooses Paul to sing.

Sentences such as (ii) require the main clause direct object to be made subject of the subordinate clause, as in the case of complements to verbs such as *tell*,

iii. Sue tells Paul to sing.

By testing both (i) and (ii), we hoped to determine if our participants distinguished between the two clause types, and are sensitive to the preposition in sentences such as (i).

Each participant acted out four tokens of each of the sentence types in (i–iii), which were interspersed with the sentences from the act-out passive follow up reported above.

There was no contrast between sentence types (ii) and (iii) (65% correct in both cases), and there was a dip in performance for sentence type (i) (25% correct). When we consider the performance of just the four individuals with DS in the follow up who were in the most advanced group with respect to performance on the simple passive in the initial act-out battery, their mean score was 50% correct for the object gap *choose* sentences such as (i) and 69% correct for the *choose* sentences without an object gap such as (ii).

the main clause or the object position of the subordinate clause. In the case of an infinitival complement to V, the ambiguity is real; in the case of an adjunct clause, the ambiguity is eliminated, given the constraint blocking questioning from within an adjunct cause. The experiment had three conditions, listed in (7). The underscores in (7) represent the two potential locations for the question word.

7a Temporal adjunct, inanimate *wh*-word:
What did the fox eat _ before whistling _?
7b Temporal adjunct, animate *wh*-word:
Who did the elephant ask _ before helping _?
7c Complement to V, animate *wh*-word:
Who did the zebra ask _to kiss_?

Example stories for conditions (7a–c) are given in (8–10),

8. Example Story for the Temporal Inanimate Condition (7a)
The fox ran down to the river.
First he ate an ice-cream cone.
Then he whistled a tune he'd heard on the radio.
The fox is a clever animal.
Question: What did the fox eat before whistling?
9. Example Story for the Temporal Animate Condition (7b)
The elephant liked to work.
She asked the tiger, "Shall I help the horse carry those heavy boxes?".
The tiger said yes, so the elephant helped the horse.
The elephant was tired at the end of it all.
Question: Who did the elephant ask before helping?
10. Example Story for the Complement to V Condition (7c)
The zebra was feeling happy.
He just wanted to hug and kiss everyone.
He asked the lion, "Shall we kiss the monkey?".
The zebra was a kind animal.
Question: Who did the zebra ask to kiss?

The complete set of materials is given in Appendix 3B. Two questionnaires were used, such that in the adverbial conditions one questionnaire used the preposition *before*, while the other used the preposition *after*. Thus the alternative form of the question for the story in (8) was 'What did the fox whistle after eating?' and the alternative form for the story in (9) was 'Who did the elephant help after asking?'. The correct answer is thus different for the *before* and *after* questions, permitting a check on whether differences in degree of transitivity (some verbs preferring a transitive structure more than others), as opposed to use of syntactic constraints, could account for the choice of answer. No difference in performance for the two forms of the questions were found.

The results of this experiment with persons with Down Syndrome are presented in Table 5.7. 'Other' responses are those that could not be scored as a main clause or subordinate clause response. Where an answer did not exactly correspond to the

Table 5.7 Down syndrome participants individual response patterns (number of responses out of 3) question experiment

	Adjunct Inanimate			Adjunct Animate			Infinitival Complement Animate		
	M	S	O	M	S	O	M	S	O
JN	3			2	1		1	2	
MN	2	1		1	1	1		1	2
KW	2		1	2	1			1	2
JF	2		1	3			2	1	
JT	3			3			3		
MT	2		1		2	1		1	2
TP	3			1	1	1	1	1	1
AV	2		1	3			2	1	
JH	2	1		3			1	2	
NF	2		1		3		1		2

M = Main clause response
S = Subordinate clause response
O = Other response

content of the story, but could reasonably be construed as referring to the object of one verb but not the other in the question, it was accepted as scorable data (for example, the response 'a song' to the question in (8) would be scored as a subordinate clause response).

We compared the Adjunct Animate condition with the Infinitival Complement condition in terms of number of main clause responses per child. The difference between the two conditions fell short of significance by sign test at the 0.05 level ($z = 1.89$, $p < 0.06$, two tail), but was consistent with the use of grammar, with a greater number of main clause responses to the Adjunct Animate condition.

The contrast between the Temporal Inanimate condition and the Infinitival Complement condition is significant by sign test ($z = 2.64$, $p < 0.009$, two tail). There are two factors that differ between the conditions (animacy of the question word and type of embedded clause) in addition to the verbs used; the Temporal Inanimate condition was included in the experiment as a check that participants were not accessing a 'parasitic gap' reading of the embedded clause. A parasitic gap is a position for the question word in the embedded clause that is dependent on questioning from the main clause,

11. * What did the fox chew the gum before swallowing _?
12. What did the fox chew _ before swallowing _ ?

Since the two predicates in the Temporal Inanimate condition were incompatible with one another as a target for the question word, a parasitic gap reading is excluded.

Table 5.8 Percentage main clause and subordinate clause responses question experiment

	DS participants			3–4 year olds			Unimpaired adults		
	M	S	O	M	S	O	M	S	O
Temporal inanimate	77	07	17	72	06	22	100	00	00
Temporal animate	60	30	10	72	14	18	96	00	04
Complement to V	27	43	30	48	41	11	33	50	17

M = main clause response
S = subordinate clause response
O = other

No difference was found between Adjunct Inanimate condition and the Adjunct Animate condition ($z = 0.71$, $p > 0.47$).

The performance of the participants with DS in this experiment is both quantitatively and qualitatively similar to that of typically developing children and unimpaired adults, as shown by the percentages of responses in Table 5.8. The performance of persons with DS on infinitival complements to V shows that they can process long-distance extraction, with over 40% of their responses corresponding to extraction of the *wh*-word from the subordinate clause. At the same time, participants with DS avoid construing a *wh*-word as extracted from an adjunct clause, although it should be noted that the block on extraction from an adjunct is less strong for the participants with DS in the case of animate question words than it is for the typically developing children and unimpaired adults.

5.3.2 *Discussion*

This experiment adds to the evidence that persons with DS compute complex syntax in the same manner as typically developing children and unimpaired adults. Goodluck et al. (1992) interpreted their results as evidence that typically developing children are aware of the constraint in English that blocks movement of a question word from within an adjunct clause. However, additional cross-linguistic work (Goodluck et al. 1995) has shown that both child and adult speakers of a language that does allow a question word to refer to a position inside an adjunct clause (Akan, spoken in Ghana) also avoid construing the question word as inside an adjunct in the ambiguous question response task (Akan speakers were given a translation of Goodluck et al's 1992 experiment). Given this cross-linguistic evidence, the results of the ambiguous question task must be construed as an effect of sentence processing, rather than a direct reflection of knowledge of language-particular rules for question formation. This follow-up experiment thus argues that persons with DS process sentences in the same manner as non-impaired individuals, with attention to the type of embedded clause involved (complement vs. adjunct).

5.4 Summary and Conclusion

The tests reported in this chapter have both deepened and extended our knowledge of the syntactic competence of some of our participants with DS. The passive tests show a difficulty with experiencer passives also found for typically developing children, and an amelioration of that difficulty when the *by*-phrase is eliminated in the judgement task. The question response task revealed a sensitivity to the type of embedded clause targeted for extraction of a question word, with a degree of discrimination similar to that found for preschool children and non-impaired adults.

References

Eriks-Brophy, A., H. Goodluck, and D. Stojanović. 2003. Sensitivity to A- and A'-bar dependencies in high functioning individuals with Down Syndrome. *Proceedings of the 27th Boston University conference on language development*, Vol 1.

Fox, D., and Y. Grodzinsky. 1998. Children's passive: A view from the *by*-phrase. *Linguistic Inquiry*, 29: 311–332.

Goodluck, H., K. Saah, and D. Stojanović. 1995. On the default mechanism for interrogative binding. *Canadian Journal of Linguistics*, 40: 377–404.

Goodluck, H., M. Foley, and J. Sedivy. 1992. Adjunct islands and acquisition. In *Island constraints: Theory, acquisition and processing*, eds. H. Goodluck, and M. Rochemont, 181–194. Dordrecht: The Netherlands.

Maratsos, M., D. Fox, J. Becker, and M. Chalkley. 1985. Semantic restrictions on children's passives. *Cognition* 19: 167–191.

Perović, A. 2006. Syntactic deficit in Down Syndrome: More evidence for the modular organization of language. *Lingua*, 116: 1616–1630.

Chapter 6
Delayed but not Deviant: A Challenge

Abstract The general 'delayed but not deviant' view of language in persons with Down Syndrome (DS) has been challenged in papers that study the comprehension of reflexive pronouns and definite pronouns in the population of DS individuals. The general consensus in the literature on typically developing child language has been that definite pronouns offer a greater challenge to the learner than reflexive pronouns, although there are exceptions. Studies of persons with DS have argued that the reverse is true for that population. We report new studies that argue that the pattern found for typically developing children is also present in the population of persons with DS. We leave an open verdict about the difference between the results of the various studies.

Keywords Delayed not deviant · Definite pronouns · Reflexive pronouns

6.1 Background

The comprehension results reported in Chap. 3 and 5 are consistent with, and supportive of, the 'delayed but not deviant' view of language development in persons with DS. The mid-2000s saw three papers on the comprehension of definite and reflexive pronouns that present a challenge for that view (Perovic 2006, 2008; Ring and Clahsen 2005). In this chapter we will summarize their findings, report a new comprehension test with nine of our participants with DS, a follow up with three of those persons, and a second follow up with two new participants. Our conclusion will be that, although there remain factors that are mysterious, the delayed but not deviant view remains viable.

6.2 Perović (2006)

Studies of the comprehension of reflexive pronouns and definite pronouns by typically developing preschool children beginning with Chien and Wexler (1990) have

H. Goodluck, *Complex Syntax in the Language of Persons with Down Syndrome*, SpringerBriefs in Linguistics,
https://doi.org/10.1007/978-3-030-96440-5_6

reported that more errors are made with the latter than with the former. Thus children have been found to correctly interpret the pronoun *herself* as referring to the subject of the sentence in (1), but may make the error of making the pronoun *her* refer to the subject in (2), when the adult grammar requires that the pronoun refer to an entity not mentioned in the sentence,

1. Snow White$_i$ is washing herself$_i$
2. Snow White$_i$ is washing her$_j$.

This has become known as the 'Delay of Principle B effect'. In the standard Binding Theory of Chomsky (1981) Principle A states that a reflexive must be bound in its local domain (for our purposes the immediately dominating sentence), whereas Principle B states that a definite pronoun must be free in its local domain, precluding coreference between *her* and *Snow White* in (2). (The accuracy of the claim that Principle B sentences are more challenging than Principle A sentences for typically developing children is taken up in Sect. 6.3).

Perović (2006) was the first to study comprehension of pronominal forms in persons with DS. She used a picture-cued truth value judgement test based on Chien and Wexler (1990), in which participants verified questions against pictures. Questions such as 'Is Snow White washing herself?' and 'Is Snow White washing her?' were presented in the context of pictures of Snow White washing herself, with someone else looking on, and of Snow White standing by while another character washes herself. All questions were presented in both Match and Mismatch conditions—e.g. the question 'Is Snow White washing herself' was presented in the context of the picture of Snow White performing a reflexive action (Match, for which the correct answer is 'Yes') and (in a separate trial) in the context of the picture of Snow White looking on while another character washes herself (Mismatch, for which the correct answer is 'No').[1]

Perović's participants with DS were four females aged between 17 and 21 and four typically developing children aged between 5;11 and 7;10 years, matched to the participants with DS on verbal mental age (based on their scores on the British Picture Vocabulary Scales).

Perović's results were striking. On both the Match and Mismatch conditions, the participants with DS did better in interpreting definite pronouns than they did in interpreting reflexive pronouns. The persons with DS made no errors whatsoever on the definite pronoun conditions (100% correct) but scored around chance on the reflexive forms, the reverse of the pattern reported in the literature for typically developing participants. (The typically developing children tested by Perović did well with both pronouns and reflexives, with never less than 75% correct. This is

[1] In addition to questions with a name in subject position, questions with a quantified NP in subject position (e.g. 'Is every bear washing himself/him?') were also tested. The prediction, based on theoretical analyses such as Grodzinsky and Reinhart (1993), and borne out by some studies with typically developing children, is that performance will be better on pronouns with quantified antecedents. The claim that quantified antecedents will reduce the error rate for pronouns for typically developing children has been challenged in experimental work by Conroy et al. (2009), and does not bear in a crucial way on the debate concerning the performance of persons with DS.

what we would expect given their ages—the Delay of Principle B effect is generally found for younger children).

6.3 Ring and Clahsen (2005)

Ring and Clahsen used a picture identification task devised by van der Lely and Stollwerck (1997) in a study of eight adolescent individuals with Down Syndrome. The structure of the test was essentially the same as that used by Perović. Ring and Clahsen also administered a picture identification test of comprehension of the passive (van der Lely 1996). Like Perović, they found more errors with reflexive pronouns than with definite pronouns, the opposite of a pattern that has been reported for typically developing children. Ring and Clahsen link this to difficulty with the passive, on a particular syntactic analysis (see below, Sect. 6.8.1).

6.4 Perović (2008)

Perović (2008) adapted her study of English-speaking subjects with DS to Serbo-Croatian. Serbo-Croatian has sets of full and clitic pronouns that are marked for person and gender. The full reflexive form *sebe* is marked for case, but not for person or gender; the clitic reflexive form *se* is invariant. The unmarked (normal) reflexive is *se*. The full reflexive *sebe* is used in emphatic/contrastive contexts (the equivalent of 'John likes HIMSELF, not Fred'). (3–4) give examples of full and clitic definite pronouns and (5–6) examples of full and clitic reflexives,

3. Marija$_i$ njega$_j$ često zove
   Maria him often calls.
   'Maria often calls him'.
4. Ovaj čovek$_i$ ga$_j$ poznaje
   This man him-clitic knows
   'This man knows him'
5. Maria$_i$ smatra sebe$_i$ paretnom
   Maria considers self-ACC clever
   'Maria considers herself clever'
6. Marco$_i$ se$_i$ brije
   Marco *se*-clitic shaves
   'Marco shaves himself'

The design of Perović's study was essentially the same as that of her English study, with additional conditions to test comprehension of clitic pronouns and reflexives, as well as full forms. Perović's subjects were six individuals with DS, aged between 19 and 29 years, and six typically developing children aged 5–6 years, matched to the DS subjects on vocabulary test scores.

The results of this study were more mixed than those of the two English studies. On Match conditions, the performance of both typically developing and DS participants was high (at ceiling for typically developing children and over 80% correct for the subjects with DS) for both full pronouns and the full reflexive *sebe*. Performance remained high on the Mismatch conditions for full pronouns and *sebe* for the typically developing children and for the DS participants in the case of pronouns. However, the performance of participants with DS on the mismatched *sebe* conditions fell to about 60%, with four of the participants doing worse with the reflexive than with pronouns. Turning to the clitic pronouns, performance for the Match conditions was high (again over 80% correct), but for the DS participants fell in the Mismatch conditions, to about 70% for the non-reflexive clitics with a quantified antecedent and to just below 80% for the reflexive clitic (see footnote 1).

6.5 A Further Test of the Pronoun/Reflexive Contrast

We sought to replicate the findings of the English studies just summarized. We designed an act-out task with sentences such as (7–8), as well as active and passive sentences such as (9–10),

7. The gorilla washes himself
8. The gorilla washes him
9. The gorilla washes the pig
10. The gorilla is washed by the pig.

Props for the experiment were a pair of gorillas (one male and one female) and a pair of pigs (one male and one female), three other animals (a lion, a bear and an elephant), a wash basin and a fence. The sex of the animal pairs (gorillas and pigs) was determined by their attire—blue shirt and trousers vs. pink dress.[2] Only the animal pairs were used in the conditions testing the binding theory; the active and passive conditions used both the animal pairs and the other animals. The complete set of materials is given in Appendix 4. The two animals to be used in the act-out (for example, the male gorilla and the male pig for 7–10) were put out by the experimenter before she read the test sentence. There were four tokens of each sentence type, with four verbs in each sentence type (*tickle*, *wash*, *pat* and *lick*).

Participants were eight of the ten DS participants who took part in the two follow ups reported in Chap. 5, and one additional participant from the original cohort reported in Chap. 3.

[2] The gender-stereotyped colours of the animals' outfits were not our choice, but what was available in toy stores.

Table 6.1 Down Syndrome participants individual response patterns (number correct out of 4) pronoun interpretation experiment

PPVT Age equivalent	Active	Passive	Reflexive	Definite Pronoun
JT 10;01	4	4	4	4
AV 8;01	4	1	4	4
JN 12;11	4	3	4	3
RF 4;06	4	1	4	1
KAW 5;03	4	1	4	2
JF 6;03	4	1	4	1
MT 9;11	4	2	3	3
MN 10;00	4	0	2	3
RM 9;05	4	0	4	0
Mean % correct	100	36	92	58

The results are given in Table 6.1, in terms of the number of correct responses each subject gave for each condition. Of the nine participants, two scored perfectly on both reflexives and definite pronouns, five had more correct responses to the reflexive condition than to the pronoun condition, with each getting all four reflexive tokens correct, and no more than two out of four correct for the definite pronoun sentences. Of the remaining two participants, one had no difference between pronouns and reflexives and the other had one more correct response for definite pronouns. Notice that three of the five participants who showed the 'typical' pattern of more errors with definite pronouns that with reflexives had the three lowest scores on the Peabody Picture Vocabulary Test (PPVT) of the nine participants (see Table 6.1), suggesting that it is not (a lack of) general intellectual development that leads to the surprising pattern found by Perović and by Ring and Clahsen (a point also made by Ring and Clahsen). Thus this test does not replicate the results of Perović and Ring and Clahsen, but rather shows the pattern of greater ease with reflexives that has been reported for typically developing children.

Thirty-six typically developing children age four to five years were tested on an act-out of the same kind as we used for the persons with DS, as part of a larger study (Goodluck 2007). Each child responded to four tokens of definite and four tokens of reflexive pronouns. Table 6.2 summarizes their performance.

Table 6.2 Distribution of responses for typically developing children pronoun interpretation experiment

Children with more correct for reflexives	Children with more correct for definite pronouns	No difference between reflexives and definite pronouns
20	8	8

As can be seen from Table 6.2, the largest group of children was those who did better on Principle A sentences than on Principle B sentences, although the reverse pattern was also found. Overall, the pattern for the typically developing children in this test is comparable to that for the individuals with DS.

6.6 An Effect of Task?

In order to check that the difference between our results with DS participants and those of Perović and of Ring and Clahsen was not an effect of the task used, we revisited three of the DS participants (the only three available) and administered a judgement task that was modelled on Perović's. The test involved a family of characters (Grandma, Grandad, Jane and Tom) and pictures in which one of the two same-sex characters either acted on himself/herself while the other character looked on, or the first character performed an action on the other character. For example, a picture of Grandad patting himself with Tom standing by should elicit a 'Yes' response to the question 'Is Grandad patting himself?' (a Match condition) and a picture of Tom patting himself with Grandad standing by should elicit a 'No' response to the same question (a Mismatch condition). There were 16 pictures in total, with eight 'Yes' responses and eight 'No' responses anticipated. The verbs used were *pat*, *wash*, *scratch* and *tickle*, each being used for a correct 'Yes' response in two cases and a correct 'No' response in two cases. The materials are given in Appendix 4.

The three persons tested were JT, JN and MN. All performed perfectly, with the exception of MN, who had one error on a sentence with a definite pronoun. Note that MN was the only participant on the act-out test that had a higher number of correct (by one) responses to pronouns than to reflexives; thus to the (minimal) extent of the data available, there was a contrast between MN's performance on the two tests.

6.7 A New Judgement Task

In an additional follow up study with two persons with DS (not included in the previous tests), we probed further the effects of task. These two individuals, like our previous participants, could read at the sentence level. They did an act-out task, the judgement task described in the previous section and a new judgement test.[3] In the new judgment test two pictures were presented side by side. For example, on the left side a picture of Grandad patting himself with Tom standing by, and on the right a picture of Grandad patting Tom, was coupled with the command 'Show me Grandad patting himself'. Thus the participant had only to point to the left hand picture to

[3] The new judgment test was equivalent to that used by Sanoudaki and Varlokosta (2014), although we were unaware of that study when we planned our test.

give a correct response. There were four pairs of pictures coupled with a command containing a reflexive pronoun and four pairs of pictures coupled with a command containing a definite pronoun. Correct answers were evenly divided between left and right pictures and sequences of correct answers of more than two left or right pictures were avoided. The complete set of materials are given in Appendix 4.

The two participants first did the act-out task, followed by the first version of the judgement task. The act-out task, in which there were four tokens of each sentence type, and the second version of the judgement task used the same verbs as the first version of the task (*pat*, *wash*, *scratch* and *tickle*). The second version of the judgement task was done about a week later than the act-out and the first judgement task.

The results are given in Table 6.3. The first child (D) consistently scored higher on the reflexive pronouns (only one error across all three tests) than on the definite pronouns. The second child's (B's) performance on the act-out resembles the pattern found by Perović and by Ring and Clahsen: trouble with the passive and reflexive pronouns and better performance (though only with one correct) on definite pronouns. B showed a pattern of preference for 'Yes' responses in the first judgement test, resulting in a 50% correct score for pronouns; the only two correct 'No' answers were given to reflexives. Despite this, in both the judgement tasks better performance was found for reflexive pronouns than for definite pronouns for the two children; the second judgement task did produce some improvement, although the amount of data is small.

Table 6.3 Results for the act-out and judgement tasks: Number correct

	Age	PPVT Age equivalent	Active	Passive	Reflexive	Pronoun
D	8;9	6;5				
Act-out			4/4 100%	1/4 25%	4/4 100%	1/4 25%
Judgement #1			–	–	7/8 87.5%	3/8 37.5%
Judgement #2			–	–	4/4 100%	2/4 50%
B	12;10	7;8				
Act-out			4/4 100%	2/4 50%	0/4 0%	1/4 25%
Judgement #1			–	–	6/8 75%	4/8 50%
Judgement #2			–	–	4/4 100%	2/4 50%

6.8 Discussion

6.8.1 The Accounts of Perović and Ring and Clahsen

Both Perović and Ring and Clahsen situate their results within accounts of proform interpretation that differ from the standard theory of Chomsky (1981). Like several researchers who have studied typically developing children, Perović draws on Reinhart and Reuland (1993), who propose that the interpretation of reflexive pronouns takes place in the syntactic component of the grammar, involving a binding relationship (a relationship in which the first element c-commands the second) between two arguments of a verb. Definite pronouns do not fall under this condition. Perović's analysis is that there is a selective grammatical deficit—an inability to establish binding relations between arguments—that affects the ability of persons with DS to interpret reflexives. Perović observes that it is consistent with this account that persons with DS (including those in Perović's study) have difficulty with the passive.

Ring and Clahsen pursue this line of reasoning, drawing on the work of Reuland (2001). Reuland argues that both passive and reflexive sentences involve the establishment of a relationship between two entities with several properties in common: both constructions involve a linking of argument positions (where argument refers to positions such as subject and object); both involve linking two entities with identical semantic features; and both involve a local linkage in which the first element is syntactically superior (c-commands) the latter:

11. Passive: The $gorilla_i$ is washed e_i

12. Reflexive: The $gorilla_i$ washes $himself_i$

On this view, it is perhaps not surprising that performance on passives and reflexives should show similar patterns, although this was not the case in our data. Table 6.1 shows that the correct responses for reflexive pronouns was 92%, compared with 58% correct for definite pronouns and 33% correct for passive sentences.

We are forced to seek an answer to why the persons with DS in our follow up behaved in a different manner to those in the Perović and the Ring and Clahsen studies.

6.8.2 Differences in Syntactic and Lexical Knowledge?

One obvious line of attack is that the subjects in the Perović and Ring and Clahsen studies and our study differed in their ability with passive—i.e. that the participants in our study were at a stage where they were doing better on the passive and (on a Reuland-type account) hence better equipped to deal with reflexives. It seems we can eliminate this as an explanation: the mean correct for the passive in our study was 33%, whereas in Ring and Clahsen's study the percentage correct on passives which included a *by*-phrase was just under 50% (Ring and Clahsen, Fig. 2), with no subject scoring less than 30%.

Knowledge of the lexical form of definite and reflexive pronouns is another candidate explanation. As mentioned above, Perović's results with Serbo-Croatian were not as clear cut as those of Perović or Ring and Clahsen with English-speaking participants. It is plausible that the Serbian results were affected by the nature of the input. The full reflexive *sebe* is a marked form that is less frequent in the language than the reflexive clitic *se*. Perović herself suggests that the success her participants with DS have with *sebe* in the Match condition, compared to their lack of success in the Mismatch condition, may be due to use of a strategy for responding—the use of a 'Yes' response based on the presence in the picture of the person named in the question. On this account, the individual uses a strategy of responding to accommodate lack of knowledge of a lexical item. Jakubowicz (1994) provides evidence of Danish-speaking children having trouble with reflexive forms that are rare in the input.

Perović also found that the performance of persons with DS was relatively good for the clitic forms, although two of her participants did poorly with non-reflexive clitics. An absence of the 'Delay of Principle B effect' with clitic pronouns has been reported in the literature for typically developing children, although the results have not been entirely consistent. McKee (1992) found high performance with both reflexive and non-reflexive clitics in typically developing Italian speakers and Goodluck et al. (1995) found similarly high performance with both reflexive and non-reflexive clitics for Serbo-Croatian speaking children, whereas in a study of Spanish children by Padilla-Rivera (1990) performance was low at younger ages, although better with reflexive clitics than with definite pronouns.

In sum, if we bear in mind the rarity of *sebe* and other results in the literature on typically developing children's interpretation of clitic pronouns, Perović's results with Serbo-Croatian do not clearly support the view that reflexives are more challenging for persons with DS than definite pronouns are.

That still leaves us with the striking results of Perović and of Ring and Clahsen with English-speaking persons with DS. One possibility, similar to that suggested above for Serbo-Croatian *sebe,* is that the English-speaking persons with DS in Perović and Ring and Clahsen's studies were not familiar with the reflexive pronoun. Ring and Clahsen argue against this possibility, on the ground that the proportion of correct responses by their DS participants was significantly higher for definite pronouns than was the proportion of incorrect responses for reflexive pronouns, a difference that could not simply be explained by the subjects simply treating reflexives as definite pronouns. (This explanation seems to us not entirely convincing, given that unfamiliarity with an item can trigger a degree of randomness in responding.) Moreover, although the DS participants in the Perović and the Ring and Clahsen studies were speakers of British English and those in our study were speakers of Canadian English (with the exception of the two individuals tested in our second judgement task), we think it is highly implausible that the two dialects differ in the frequency of input of reflexive forms, making unfamiliarity with the reflexive forms a poor candidate for an explanation of the patterns of data.

6.9 The Generality of the Asymmetry Between Pronouns and Reflexives

Perović and Ring and Clahsen assume that the child language studies of typically developing children never show an advantage of reflexives over definite pronouns:

> This pattern is not documented at any stage in typical language development… as reported for English in Jakubowicz (1984), Chien and Wexler (1990) or other languages in studies which focused on typical acquisition of binding... (Perović, p. 1624)

> It is also worth mentioning that the dissociation found in DS between correct non-reflexive and impaired reflexive pronoun interpretation has not been witnessed before in any studies of syntactic binding with unimpaired children of any age. (Ring and Clahsen, p. 494)

However, it is more correct to say that the difficulty with reflexives is less frequent than difficulty with pronouns for typically developing children. Kaufman (1994) surveyed the literature on comprehension of definite and reflexive pronouns at that point in time (see Kaufman 1994, Tables 7.1 and 7.4). Although the overall picture presented there is one of greater difficulty with definite pronouns, that pattern was not invariant. Act-out is the only task of those used (act-out, truth value judgement, and picture selection) in which there are instances in which some typically developing children do worse on reflexives than on definite pronouns, although overall there is clearly still an advantage of reflexive pronouns. Moreover, the performance of typically developing children reported above (Table 6.2) confirms that greater difficulty with definite pronouns is not an invariant pattern. In the one study that Kaufman lists that employed both act out and truth value judgement (Sigurjónsdóttir and Hyams 1992), a (small) advantage was found for definite pronouns in the act-out task, and an advantage for reflexives in the truth value judgement task. In a more recent survey of the literature, Conroy et al. (2009) conclude that the 'Delay of Principle B' effect has been exaggerated, due to flaws in the design of truth value judgement tasks.

So where does this leave us in evaluating the conflicting evidence from the studies of English-speaking persons with DS? A simple appeal to the task that was used is not going to work: although there have been cases of typically developing children doing worse with reflexives than with definite pronouns, those cases have involved the act-out task, not the truth value judgement task—the opposite of what we would expect from the three studies by Perović and Ring and Clahsen. The best we can say at this point is that the literature on typically developing children does not indicate invariably an advantage for reflexive pronouns, or an advantage as large as has been claimed in the literature (Conroy et al. 2009).

With respect to the analyses adopted by Perović and by Ring and Clahsen, it would be helpful to know if there is a stage of processing during which the computation of relations between the subject position and object position (either as a reflexive pronoun or the trace of a passive structure) takes place. Although there is evidence in the adult processing literature in favour of the reality of movement in passive sentences and in favour of immediate binding of a reflexive to a subject, there is no clear indication that this takes place at a unified stage. However, the analyses of Perović and Ring and Clahsen are convincing for the data presented in those articles.

In an article subsequent to those reported above, Sanoudaki and Varlokosta (2014) report that Greek-speakers with Down Syndrome perform worse than typically developing children on reflexive pronouns.[4] One possibility that Sanoudaki and Varlokosta consider is that the persons with DS were older in their study than those in a previous study (23 to 34 years) that showed no difference between reflexives and definite pronouns (Stathopoulou 2009), allowing for development beyond the level reached in the previous study, and a deficit with reflexives to show up. Given that the two persons who scored perfectly on reflexive and definite pronouns on our test (Table 6.1, JT and AV) had chronological ages of 33 years and 18 years, and the ages of the remaining persons in that table ranged between 10 and 32 years, this seems unlikely as a potential explanation.

6.10 Conclusion

At this point, it appears that the most sensible position concerning the claim that persons with DS show a deviant pattern of grammatical development with respect to the interpretation of definite and reflexive pronouns is to enter the Scottish verdict 'Not Proven'. The data thus far gathered by Perović, Ring and Clahsen and Sanoudaki and Varlokosta stand in contrast to the other evidence presented in Chap. 2, 3 and 4 that support the 'delayed but not deviant' view of language development in DS, and to the studies of study of pronouns and reflexives reported in this chapter. We have seen that typically developing children do on occasion find reflexives more difficult than definite pronouns, although the potential reasons for this pattern (task based or lexical knowledge of proforms) remain obscure. The perfect performance of two participants in our act-out task (JT and AV) on reflexive and definite pronouns, the pattern of greater difficulty with definite pronouns for five of the remaining participants in the first judgement test, and the performance of the two individuals who did both judgement tasks, stands as testimony that the genetic disorder of DS

[4] It should be noted that although the individuals with DS performed worse with reflexive pronouns than typically developing children did, the results of the study did not follow a clear-cut pattern. Two puzzles are present in the data. The first is that while persons with DS performed worse on simple sentences with reflexives, they performed at the same level as typically developing children when there were two antecedents for the reflexive (the equivalent of *The queen next to the witch is drawing herself*), which a previous study has shown to be difficult for typically developing children (Varlokosta 2001, reported in Sanoudaki and Varlokosta 2014); it might be expected that the persons with DS would do worse than typically developing children. Error rates for both groups were high, and so no real conclusion can be drawn from this first apparent anomaly. Second, adults who were also tested made a substantial (and statistically significant) number of errors with sentences with pronouns; this may be due to the task of picture selection (Sanoudaki and Varlokosta 2015).

does not entail an insurmountable obstacle to the pattern of language development found for typically developing children.[5]

References

Chien, Y.-C., and K. Wexler. 1990. Children's knowledge of locality restrictions on binding as evidence for the modularity of syntax and pragmatics. *Language Acquisition* 1: 225–295.

Chomsky, N. 1981. *Lectures on government and binding.* Dordrecht, The Netherlands: Foris.

Conroy, A., E. Takahashi, J. Lidz, and C. Philips. 2009. Equal treatment for all antecedents: How children succeed with Principle B. *Linguistic Inquiry* 40: 446–486.

Goodluck, H. 2007. Exposure, implicit instruction and the development of a late-acquired construction. *York Papers in Linguistics.*

Goodluck, H., K. Saah, and D. Stojanović. 1995. On the default mechanism for interrogative binding. *Canadian Journal of Linguistics* 40: 377–404.

Grodzinsky, Y., and T. Reinhart. 1993. The innateness of binding and coreference. *Linguistic Inquiry* 24: 69–101.

Jakubowicz, C. 1994. Reflexives in French and Danish: Morphology, syntax and acquisition. In *Syntactic theory and first language acquisition: Cross linguistic perspectives*, eds. B. Lust, G. Hermon and J. Kornfilt. *Volume 2: Binding, dependencies and learnability*, 115–144. Hillsdale NJ: Lawrence Erlbaum Associates.

Kaufman, D. 1994. Grammatical or pragmatic: Will the real principle B please stand up? In *Syntactic theory and first language acquisition: Cross linguistic perspectives*, eds. B. Lust, G. Hermon and J. Kornfilt. *Volume 2: Binding, dependencies and learnability.* Hillsdale, NJ: Lawrence Erlbaum Associates.

McKee, C. 1992. A comparison of pronouns and anaphors in Italian and English acquisition. *Language Acquisition* 2: 21–54.

Padilla-Rivera, J. 1990. *On the definition of binding domains in Spanish.* Dordrecht, The Netherlands: Kluwer.

Perović, A. 2006. Syntactic deficit in Down Syndrome: More evidence for the modular organization of language. *Lingua* 116: 1616–1630.

Perović, A. 2008. A cross-linguistic analysis of binding in Down Syndrome. In *First language acquisition of morphology and syntax*, eds. P. Guijarro-Fuentes, M. Pilar Larranage and J. Clibbens. Amsterdam, The Netherlands: John Benjamins.

Reinhart, T., and E. Reuland. 1993. Reflexivity. *Linguistic Inquiry* 24: 657–720.

Reuland, E. 2001. Primitives of binding. *Linguistic Inquiry* 32: 439–492.

Ring, M., and H. Clahsen. 2005. Distinct patterns of language impairment in Down's syndrome and Williams syndrome: The case of syntactic chains. *Journal of Neurolinguistics* 18: 479–501.

Sanoudaki, E., and S. Varlokosta. 2014. Pronoun comprehension in individuals with Down Syndrome: Deviance or delay? *Journal of Speech, Language and Hearing Research* 57: 1442–1452.

Sanoudaki, E., and S. Varlokosta. 2015. Task effects in the interpretation of pronouns. *Language Acquisition* 22: 40–67.

Sigurjónsdóttir, S., and N. Hyams. 1992. Reflexivization and logophoricity: Evidence from the acquisition of Icelandic. *Language Acquisition* 2: 359–413.

[5] See Chap. 7 for discussion of the problem of matching performance for typically developing children and persons with DS.

Stathopoulou, E. 2009. Written mediation in KPG exams: Source text regulation resulting in hybrid formation. Unpublished MA dissertation, Faulty of English Language and Literature, National and Kapodistrian University of Athens.

van der Lely, H. 1996. Specifically language impaired and normally developing children: Verbal passive vs. adjectival sentence interpretation. *Lingua* 98: 243–272.

van der Lely, H., and L. Stollwerck. 1997. Binding theory and specifically language impaired children. *Cognition* 62: 245–290.

Varlokosta, S. 2001. On the acquisition of pronominal and reflexive clitics in child Greek. In *Research on Child Language Acquisition*, eds. A. Almgren, A. Barreña, M.-J. Ezeizabarrena, I. Idiazabal and B. MacWhinney, 1383–1400. Somerville, MA: Cascadilla Press.

Chapter 7
Conclusion: Some Prospects for Research into Syntax in Persons with Down Syndrome

Abstract The results of Chap. 2–7 are briefly summarised, focusing on both the similarities and contrasts between typically developing children and typical adults and persons with Down Syndrome (DS). The chapter then considers unresolved questions: the role of standardized tests in evaluating persons with DS, and the causal link between the ability to read and the ability to master linguistic complexities.

Keywords Similarities/differences · DS vs. typically developing children · Standardized tests · Reading

7.1 Summary of Results

We have seen that persons with DS display both similarities and differences in comparison to typically developing children and typical adults. First, consider the similarities. Persons with DS in this study show in some respects an overall pattern of increasing difficulty for the ten constructions considered in Chaps. 2 and 3; that pattern overall accords with the degree of difficulty found for those constructions in typically developing children between 4 and 12 years. When we compared the performance of the individuals with DS on pairs of constructions that differ by one factor, we found patterns that reflected English grammar, i.e. individuals with DS showed a pattern of correct responses to both (1) and (2), (1) and (3), and (4) and (5), although the error rates were high and the patterns were established only when the data was adjusted to eliminate uninformative responses,

1. Sue tells Paul$_i$ [PRO$_i$ to kiss Mom] (Paul kisses)
2. Sue$_i$ is told by Paul [PRO$_i$ to kiss Mom] (Sue kisses)
3. Sue$_i$ promised Paul [PRO$_i$ to kiss Mom] (Sue kisses)
4. Sue$_i$ is eager [PRO$_i$ to kiss] (Sue kisses)
5. Sue$_i$ is easy [PRO to kiss e$_i$] (Sue is kissed)

H. Goodluck, *Complex Syntax in the Language of Persons with Down Syndrome*, SpringerBriefs in Linguistics,
https://doi.org/10.1007/978-3-030-96440-5_7

Chapter 4 concerned production. We showed that the persons with DS studied in Chap. 3 produced a range of complex syntactic structures, which increased numerically with the age of the participants. We also showed that there was a varied vocabulary of key items (for example, verbs that take infinitival and tensed complements), indicating that the structures produced were not limited to particular words.

We found in Chap. 5 that persons with DS also show a similarity to typically developing children aged 4–5 with respect to the difficulty of passive sentences, being sensitive to presence/absence of a *by*-phrase when the verb is one that has an experiencer subject in the active voice, i.e. persons with DS were more successful in interpreting sentences such as (6) than they were in interpreting (7),

6. Dad was heard in the kitchen
7. Dad was heard by Mom

Also in Chap. 5, persons with DS behaved in a very similar manner to both 4–5 year old children and typical adults in their responses to questions that targeted positions within a complement to V and an adverbial clause: they permitted reference to a position inside a complement to V (8), but eschewed reference to a position inside an adverbial clause (9),

8. Who did the zebra ask to kiss?
9. Who did the elephant ask before helping?

We argued that this was a sentence processing effect, rather than sensitivity of the grammar of English.

In Chap. 6, we showed that persons with DS had greater difficulty with definite pronouns that with reflexive pronouns, permitting a definite pronoun to refer to the subject of the same sentence, which is ungrammatical in adult English. A similar pattern of error has been found for some typically developing preschool children. This similarity to preschool children runs against the findings of other studies of persons with DS, which report greater error in the case of reflexive pronouns (Perović 2006; Ring and Clahsen 2005).

We turn now to differences between our individuals with DS and typically developing children. When asked to identify the missing subject of an infinitival complement to *promise*, typically developing children show an abrupt shift from an incorrect object of the main clause response at age 4–5 to a correct subject of the main clause response at age 6–7. No such sudden shift was found for persons with DS at age equivalences established by the PPVT, despite the fact that the group with DS did show sensitivity to the contrast between the complement to *tell* type verbs and *promise* (1 vs. 3). We also showed a contrast reflecting knowledge of English grammar in the interpretations given by persons with DS to the infinitive complements to *eager* vs. *easy*, (4) vs. (5), but we found no evidence that a certain predicate or predicates led the way for the more difficult *easy*; this is in contrast to the typically developing children we tested (Chap. 2), who were found at age 4–5 to do better with one predicate for the *easy* construction, and to the results of McKee (1997).

We found in the act-out task reported in Chap. 2 clear patterns for some typically developing children in the 4–5 year old age group of use of an agent strategy or a patient strategy in interpreting the null subject of a temporal adjunct clause; no clear evidence of such strategies was found in the act-out task for persons with DS, although there was evidence of the use of such strategies in the written task. The largest group of persons with DS in the written task adopted a strategy of reference to the linearly closest NP in the main clause (no data is available for typically developing children for a written task).

7.2 Puzzles and Directions for Future Research

This research has raised questions that we can only broach here. The first is the efficacy of standardized tests in evaluating and predicting performance; this has long been recognised as a challenge facing researchers (see Chapman 1997, p. 308). Our data raises some anomalies which deserve more consideration. There is the contrast in performance of JT and MT in production reported in Chap. 4. The scores on standardized tests were similar for these two individuals, but their behaviour was markedly different in the elicited story telling task (a short coherent story with relatively limited complex syntax vs. a rather long story that was not always to point, with a range of complex syntactic structures).

Another case of the possible inadequacy of standardized tests is the data on pronouns and reflexives reported in Chap. 6. Perović (2006) matched her participants with DS to typically developing children based on their scores on verbal mental age, as measured by the British Picture Vocabulary Scales. As noted in Sect. 7.1 above, the results of the Perović study revealed a pattern for persons with DS that differed from that found in many studies of typically developing children: typically developing children generally have more difficulty with definite pronouns than with reflexive pronouns, but the opposite was true for persons with DS in the study by Perović. The same was true in the study by Ring and Clahsen (2005), who matched the participants with DS to typically developing children by a correspondence between mental age of participants with DS (based on Wechsler 1992) and the chronological age of the children. In our experiments, the pattern of greater ease with reflexives was found for persons with DS, contrary to the results of Perović and of Ring and Clahsen. We questioned in Chap. 6 the claim that the pattern of greater ease with reflexive pronouns was invariably true for typically developing children, and it remains an open question what the appropriate measures are on which persons with DS can be matched to typically developing children.

Another major question that we cannot address on the basis of our data is the relationship between reading and language development. Is it the case that the persons with DS that we studied had a particular ability that both allowed them to succeed in learning to read and in producing and comprehending language? Or is it that the ability to read prompted language growth? A causal link between reading and language growth would be the most desirable outcome, and is supported by research such as that of Buckley and Bird (1993) and Buckley et al. (1996). But the question of causation is a secondary consideration: reading just makes life better.

References

Buckley S., G. Bird, and A. Byrne. 1996. The practical and theoretical significance of teaching literacy skills to children with Down syndrome. In *Down Syndrome: Psychological, psychobiological and socioeducational perspectives*, eds. J. Rondal, and J. Perera, 119–128. London, England: Whurr.

Buckley, S., and G. Bird. 1993. Teaching children with Down Syndrome to read. *Down Syndrome Research and Practice* 1: 34–39.

Chapman, R. 1997. Language development in children and adolescents with Down Syndrome. *Mental Retardation and Developmental Disabilities Research Reviews* 3: 307–312.

McKee, C. 1997. Some adjectives are 'easy' and some are not. *Lexicology* 3: 59–83.

Perović, A. 2006. Syntactic deficit in Down Syndrome: More evidence for the modular organization of language. *Lingua* 116: 1616–1630.

Ring, M., and H. Clahsen. 2005. Distinct patterns of language impairment in Down's syndrome and Williams syndrome: The case of syntactic chains. *Journal of Neurolinguistics* 18: 479–501.

Wechsler, D. 1992. *Wechsler intelligence scale for children, Third Edition UK*. Harcourt Brace and Co: The Psychological Corporation, Sidcup, Kent.

Appendix 1
Standardized Test Results, Participants with DS

Peabody Picture Vocabulary Test (PPVT)

Participant	Chronological age	Raw score	Standard score	Age equivalent	Grouping Chapter 3
1. RM	18;03	124	73	9;05	2
2. MT	32;01	127	70	9;11	3
3. JF	11;05	83	64	6;03	1
4. JT	33;10	129	71	10;01	3
5. JN	30;11	149	81	12;11	3
6. MN	24;02	128	71	10;00	3
7. K-AW	19;04	69	40	5;03	1
8. TP	22;05	98	45	7;03	2
9. AV	18;10	109	61	8;01	2
10. PO	25;11	95	41	7;00	2
11. MR	16;02	75	40	5;08	1
12. SZ	14;10	76	41	5;09	1
13. YI	19;07	81	40	6;01	1
14. RH	25;10	111	55	8;03	2
15. SB	17;01	90	47	6;08	2
16. MM	8;03	90	83	6;08	2
17. JP	21;05	73	40	5;06	1
18. SS	12;10	94	69	7;00	2
19. NF	11;00	90	69	6;08	1
20. RF	10;11	58	48	4;06	1
21. AL	17;05	110	65	8;02	2
22. JH	13;00	110	73	8;02	2

(continued)

H. Goodluck, *Complex Syntax in the Language of Persons with Down Syndrome*, SpringerBriefs in Linguistics,
https://doi.org/10.1007/978-3-030-96440-5

(continued)

Participant	Chronological age	Raw score	Standard score	Age equivalent	Grouping Chapter 3
23. JN	18;00	127	75	9;08	3
24. SL	14;05	64	40	4;11	1
25. JW	19;11	103	54	7;07	2

Gates-MacGinitie reading test

Participant (Level-form)		Raw score	GE
1. RM	Vocabulary	43	3.3
(A-3)	Comprehension	43	3.5
	Total	86	3.4
2. MT	Vocabulary	27	2.5
(B-3)	Comprehension	20	1.9
	Total	47	2.2
3. JF	Vocabulary	24	2.4
(B-3)	Comprehension	23	2.0
	Total	47	2.2
4. JT	Vocabulary	30	3.7
(C-3)	Comprehension	23	3.1
	Total	53	3.4
5. JN	Vocabulary	37	4.6
(C-3)	Comprehension	39	5.4
	Total	76	4.8
6. MN	Vocabulary	36	4.5
(C-3)	Comprehension	23	3.1
	Total	59	3.6
7. K-AW	Vocabulary	36	2.5
(A-3)	Comprehension	33	2.2
	Total	69	2.4
8. TP	Vocabulary	25	3.3
(C-3)	Comprehension	21	2.7
	Total	46	3.1
9. AV	Vocabulary	22	2.2
(B-3)	Comprehension	31	2.5
	Total	53	2.4
10. PO	Vocabulary	43	3.3
(A-3)	Comprehension	41	2.7

(continued)

(continued)

Participant (Level-form)		Raw score	GE
	Total	84	2.8
11. MR	Vocabulary	32	3.0
(B-3)	Comprehension	26	2.2
	Total	58	2.5
12. SZ	Vocabulary	41	2.9
(A-3)	Comprehension	25	1.8
	Total	66	2.3
13. YI	Vocabulary	37	2.5
(A-3)	Comprehension	24	1.8
	Total	61	2.0
14. RH	Vocabulary	34	3.2
(B-3)	Comprehension	14	1.5
	Total	48	2.2
15. SB	Vocabulary	40	3.9
(B-3)	Comprehension	44	5.2
	Total	84	4.4
(C-3)	Vocabulary	42	6.1
	Comprehension	22	2.8
	Total	64	3.9
16. MM	Vocabulary	44	3.6
(A-3)	Comprehension	37	2.4
	Total	81	2.7
17. JP	Vocabulary	41	2.9
(A-3)	Comprehension	43	3.5
	Total	84	2.8
18. SS	Vocabulary	38	3.6
(B-3)	Comprehension	21	2.0
	Total	59	2.5
19. NF	Vocabulary	23	2.3
(B-3)	Comprehension	36	2.9
	Total	59	2.5
20. RF	Subtest 1	15	
	Subtest 2	13	
	Subtest 3	12	
	Subtest 4	13	
	Total	53	2.0

(continued)

(continued)

Participant (Level-form)		Raw score	GE
21. AL	Vocabulary	22	1.7
(A-3)	Comprehension	25	1.8
	Total	47	1.8
22. JH	Vocabulary	45	6.5
(B-3)	Comprehension	38	3.2
	Total	82	4.0
(C-3)	Vocabulary	29	3.6
	Comprehension	35	4.5
	Total	64	3.9
23. JN	Vocabulary	24	3.2
(C-3)	Comprehension	28	3.5
	Total	52	3.3
(D4-3)	Vocabulary	18	3.4
	Comprehension	13	2.4
	Total	31	3.0
24. SL	Vocabulary	41	2.9
	Comprehension	28	2.0
	Total	69	2.4
25. JW	Vocabulary	43	4.8
(B-4)	Comprehension	43	5.2
	Total	87	5.3

Test for Auditory Comprehension of Language (TACL) Raw Scores

Participant	Word classes and relations (/40)	Grammatical morphemes (/40)	Elaborated sentences (/40)	Total score (/120)
1. RM	36	27	34	97
2. MT	38	19	14	71
3. JF	32	16	16	64
4. JT	35	20	19	74
5. JN	39	23	30	92
6. MN	40	28	19	87
7. K-AW	36	28	11	75
8. TP	37	31	28	96
9. AV	34	26	30	90

(continued)

(continued)

Participant	Word classes and relations (/40)	Grammatical morphemes (/40)	Elaborated sentences (/40)	Total score (/120)
10. PO	32	27	22	81
11. MR	34	27	23	84
12. SZ	28	26	15	69
13. YI	34	26	25	85
14. RH	33	82	24	82
15. SB	39	24	23	86
16. MM	27	24	27	78
17. JP	31	19	16	66
18. SS	34	24	24	82
19. NF	32	28	24	84
20. RF	27	22	17	66
21. AL	32	23	24	79
22. JH	36	20	26	82
23. JN	37	34	30	101
24. SL	28	19	9	56
25. JW	29	19	19	67

Appendix 2
Test Sentences—Act-Out and Written Tests

Act-out

Numbers in parentheses indicate the testing session

Simple active

Mom kisses Dad (1)
Paul bumps Sue (1)
Sue hugs Paul (2)
The dog pats the cat (2)
Dad tickles Sue (3)
Paul touches Sue (3)

Simple passive

Sue is pushed by Paul (1)
Mom is hugged by Dad (1)
Dad is bumped by Mom (2)
Paul is kissed by Sue (2)
The dog is licked by the cat (3)
Dad is tickled by Mom (3)

Complement to tell, active main clause

Mom asks Dad to run around the block (1)
Sue tells Paul to tickle Mom (1)
Paul tells Sue to jump the fence (2)
Dad asks Mom to jump towards Sue (2)

Complement to tell, passive main clause

Paul is told by Sue to eat a banana (1)
Dad is asked by Mom to sing to Sue (1)
Sue is told by Paul to kiss Dad (2)
Mom is asked by Dad to climb over the fence (2)

H. Goodluck, *Complex Syntax in the Language of Persons with Down Syndrome*, SpringerBriefs in Linguistics,
https://doi.org/10.1007/978-3-030-96440-5

Complement to promise

Sue promises Paul to climb over the wall (1)
Dad promises Mom to tickle Sue (2)
Paul promises Sue to jump the fence (2)
Mom promises Dad to sing to Paul (3)

Eager predicates

The cat is glad to bite (1)
Mom is eager to hug (2)
Paul is happy to kiss (2)
Dad is keen to tickle (3)

Easy predicates

Dad is tough to lift (1)
Sue is easy to kiss (2)
Mom is hard to catch (2)
Paul is fun to chase (3)

Temporal adjunct clause, main clause active

Sue tickles Dad before running towards Paul (2)
Paul chases Sue before jumping the fence (3)
The dog bites Paul after knocking down Mom (3)
Mom kisses Dad after walking round the block (3)

Temporal adjunct clause, main clause passive

Mom is tickled by Sue before running up to Dad (2)
Paul is hugged by Dad after kissing Sue (3)
Dad is chased by Sue before hiding behind the wall (3)
The cat is licked by the dog after pushing over the fence (3)

Complement to choose, object of preposition gap

Mom picks Dad to run towards (3)
Sue chooses Paul to read to (3)
Dad chooses Mom to sing to (3)
Paul picks Sue to dance with (3)

Written

Simple active

The dog pats the cat

Who pats? the dog ☐ the cat ☐ (1)

Sue hugs Paul

Who hugs? Paul ☐ Sue ☐ (1)

The boy tickles the girl

Who tickles? the boy ☐ the girl ☐ (2)

The teacher embraces the child

Who embraces? the child ☐ the teacher ☐ (2)

The farmer chases the dog

Who chases? the dog ☐ the farmer ☐ (3)

Mary calls John

Who calls? Mary ☐ John ☐ (3)

Simple passive

The cat is chased by Allison

Who chases? Allison ☐ the cat ☐ (1)

The dog is licked by the cat

Who licks? the dog ☐ the cat ☐ (1)

Dad is bumped by Mom

Who bumps? Dad ☐ Mom ☐ (2)

The woman is embraced by the child

Who embraces? the child ☐ the woman ☐ (2)

Paul is tickled by Mom

Who tickles? Mom ☐ Paul ☐ (3)

Tina is called by Ralph

Who calls? Tina ☐ Ralph ☐ (3)

Complement to tell, active main clause

Bill asks Allison to shout at Fred

Who shouts at Fred?	Bill □	Allison □ (1)

Mom asks Dad to run around the block

Who runs around the block?	Dad □	Mom □ (1)

Tina tells Tony to bring the box

Who brings the box?	Tina □	Tony □ (2)

Paul tells Bill to kiss Cathy

Who kisses Cathy?	Bill □	Paul □ (2)

Complement to tell, passive main clause

Dad is asked by Mom to sing to Sue

Who sings to Sue?	Mom □	Dad □ (1)

Bill is asked by Tina to go to the store

Who goes to the store?	Bill □	Tina □ (1)

Allison is told by Dad to open the door

Who opens the door?	Allison □	Dad □ (2)

Cathy is told by Ralph to pat the dog

Who pats the dog?	Ralph □	Cathy □ (2)

Complement to promise

Allison promises Cathy to read to Bill

Who reads to Bill?	Allison □	Cathy □ (1)

Bill promises Tina to feed the baby

Who feeds the baby?	Tina □	Bill □ (2)

Sue promises Paul to climb over the wall

Who climbs over the wall?	Sue □	Paul □ (2)

Richard promises the teacher to eat the banana

Who eats the banana?	the teacher □	Richard □ (3)

Eager predicates

The dog is eager to please

What happens?	someone pleases the dog □
	the dog pleases someone □ (1)

The fish is happy to eat

What happens?	the fish eats someone □
	someone eats the fish □ (2)

The cat is glad to bite

What happens?	the cat bites someone □
	someone bites the cat □ (2)

Mom is keen to touch

What happens?	someone touches Mom □
	Mom touches someone □ (3)

Easy predicates

The monkey is difficult to find

What happens? someone searches for the monkey □

the monkey searches for someone □ (1)

Dad is easy to hug

What happens? someone hugs dad □

Dad hugs someone □ (2)

Mom is exciting to dress

What happens? Mom dresses someone □

someone dresses Mom □ (2)

Paul is fun to chase

What happens? Paul chases someone □

someone chases Paul □ (3)

Temporal adjunct clause, main clause active

Ralph hugs Amanda before going to bed

Who goes to bed? Amanda □ Ralph □ (2)

Paul chases Sue before jumping the fence

Who jumps the fence? Sue □ Paul □ (3)

The mother meets the teacher after talking to Paul

Who talks to Paul? the mother □ the teacher □ (3)

Dad kisses Mom after hugging Tony

Who hugs Tony? Dad □ Mom □ (3)

Temporal adjunct clause, main clause passive

Cathy is hugged by Bill after speaking to the nurse

Who speaks to the nurse? Bill □ Cathy □ (2)

John is kissed by Tina before picking up the kids

Who picks up the kids? John □ Tina □ (3)

Dad is chased by Sue before hiding behind the wall

Who hides behind the wall? Dad □ Sue □ (3)

Tony is met by Peter after leaving the restaurant

Who leaves the restaurant? Tony □ Peter □ (3)

Complement to choose, object of preposition gap

Bill picks Cathy to smile at

What happens? Bill smiles at Cathy □

Cathy smiles at Bill □ (3)

Jane chooses Mom to whisper to

What happens? Mom whispers to Jane □

Jane whispers to Mom □ (3)

Dad chooses Mom to sing to

What happens? Dad sings to Mom □

Mom sings to Dad □ (3)

Sarah chooses Tina to wave at

What happens? Tina waves at Sarah □

Sarah waves at Tina □ (3)

Appendix 3
Materials—Follow-up Experiments

A. Experiments on the passive

Act-out

Active actional

Pail tickles Sue
Sue touches Paul
Mom chases Dad
Dad bumps Mom

Passive actional

Paul is bumped by Sue
Mom is tickled by Dad
Sue is chased by Paul
Dad is touched by Mom

Non-actional active

Sue hears Dad near the block
Dad sees Sue behind the fence
Paul sees the rabbit on the lawn
Mom hears Paul on the road

Non-actional passive +by

Mom is seen by Sue
Paul is heard by Dad
Dad is heard by Mom
The cat is seen by the rabbit

H. Goodluck, *Complex Syntax in the Language of Persons with Down Syndrome*, SpringerBriefs in Linguistics,
https://doi.org/10.1007/978-3-030-96440-5

Non-actional passive –by

The rabbit is seen on the lawn
Sue is seen behind the block
Paul is seen near the fence
Mom is heard on the road

Truth value judgment

Active, action verb

Paul teases Sue all the time about being a cry baby. Sue wants to show Paul she is a big girl. She tried never to cry. Paul tells her "I will make you cry". Then he starts to tickle her. He doesn't stop until he sees tears roll down her cheeks.

Match: Paul tickled Sue (Questionnaire 1)
Mismatch: Sue tickled Paul (Questionnaire 2)

Sue and Paul are playing ball outside. Sue throws the ball very far. Paul runs to try to catch the ball. He falls and hurts his knee. Then he starts to cry. Sue feels bad. She gives him a big hug. Paul is happy to have a sister like Sue.

Match: Sue hugged Paul (Q2)
Mismatch: Paul hugged Sue (Q1)

Mom has just made some eggs. Dad smells a delicious smell. He goes into the kitchen to see what Mom is making. He sees the warm eggs. He grabs the pan and runs away. Mom chases him. She wants to get the eggs back.

Match: Mom chased Dad (Q1)
Mismatch: Dad chases Mom (Q2)

Dad is having a bad day. He is tired and clumsy. First he bumps into the fence and falls down. Next he tries to eat a banana and drops it on the floor. Then he wants to go around Mom but bumps into her instead. That's it. Dad has to have a rest.

Match: Dad bumped Mom (Q2)
Mismatch: Mom bumped Dad (Q1)

Passive, action verb

Sue is just learning how to ride a bike. Paul is teaching her. Paul tells Sue to ride over to him. Sue tries, but she doesn't know how to stop. She bumps into her brother. They both fall. Paul and Sue burst out laughing.

Match: Paul was bumped by Sue (Q2)
Mismatch: Sue was bumped by Paul (Q1)

Mom seems to be very tired today. She is in a bad mood. Dad says, "I am going to cheer you up". He comes and starts to tickle her. Mom can't stop laughing. She is not in a bad mood any more.

Match: Mom was ticked by Dad (Q1)
Mismatch: Dad was tickled by Mom (Q2)

Today is Mom's birthday. Dad gives Mom a present. Mom opens it and smiles. She takes a shiny gold necklace out of the box. She puts it on and hugs Dad. Mom loves her birthday present.

Match: Dad was hugged by Mom (Q2)
Mismatch: Mom was hugged by Dad (Q1)

Mom bought herself a new hat. Sue wants to try it on, but Paul wants to try it on, too. Sue grabs it first and tries to put it on. Paul is upset. Sue runs around laughing with the hat. Paul starts chasing his sister. Then he runs to tell Mom.

Match: Sue was chased by Paul (Q1)
Mismatch: Paul was chased by Sue (Q2)

Active, experiencer verb

Dad wants to go for a walk. He asks Paul and Sue to come along, but they both say no. Dad goes out for a walk alone. Sue decides to follow Dad. Near the fence, Dad falls and hurts his leg. Dad calls "Help, help". Sue hears Dad calling for help. She runs to find him.

Match: Sue heard Dad near the fence (Q1)
Mismatch: Dad heard Sue near the fence (Q2)

Mom is sick. Dad tells Paul to keep quiet so Mom can sleep. Paul goes outside to play with his friends. They play on the road and make a lot of noise. Mom wakes up and asks Dad "What is all that noise?".

Match: Mom heard Paul on the road (Q1)
Mismatch: Paul heard Mom on the road (Q2)

Dad and the kids are playing hide and seek. Paul hides behind a tree, but Dad has no trouble spotting him. He is still looking for Sue. Dad sees shoes behind the wall. He shouts, "I know where Sue is. She's hiding behind the wall!". Then Sue tries to run away.

Match: Dad saw Sue behind the wall (Q2)
Mismatch: Sue saw Dad behind the wall (Q1)

Paul and Sue love their pet cat. Their neighbours' dog is mean, so the cat is not allowed outside the house. One day the cat is missing. Then Paul looks out of the window and screams, "The cat is on the lawn!". Dad runs to get the cat.

Match: Paul saw the cat on the lawn (Q2)
Mismatch: The cat saw Paul on the lawn (Q1)

Passive, experiencer verb, +by.

Paul is taking music at school. They are learning a lot of songs. Paul is very shy. He does not want to sing in front of his family. One day Dad heard Paul singing outside. When Paul comes in, Dad is smiling, but he doesn't say anything.

Match: Paul was heard by Dad (Q2)
Mismatch: Dad was heard by Paul (Q1)

One day Mom is alone at home. She plays some music and dances all day long. Sue comes home and hears the music. She looks through the window and sees her mother dancing. She tells Mom "You are a beautiful dancer!".

Match: Mom was seen by Sue (Q1)
Mismatch: Sue was seen by Mom (Q2)

Mom has decided that no one in the house will drink pop. One night, Dad sneaks out of the bedroom to get some pop. By mistake, Dad drops the bottle on the floor. Mom hears Dad making noise and wakes up. Dad is cleaning up the mess when Mom walks into the room.

Match: Dad was heard by Mom (Q2)
Mismatch: Mom was heard by Dad (Q1)

The cat and the pig are good friends. They share everything. One day, the cat decides she will get an ice cream. She doesn't have much money, so she does not invite the pig to come along. On her way home, she meets the pig. The pig sees the cat eating the ice cream. The pig feels sad.

Match: The cat was seen by the pig (Q1)
Mismatch: The pig was seen by the cat (Q2)

Passive, experiencer verb, −by

Paul and Sue are playing outside. They hear Mom calling them to come and eat. Sue isn't hungry. She doesn't want to go in yet. Sue hides behind the block. Mom looks out and sees Sue hiding. "Come on in", she says. "It's time for dinner now".

Match: Sue was seen behind the block (Q2)
Mismatch: Mom was seen behind the block (Q1)

Every day, Dad goes to the barn to feed his pig acorns. One day Dad goes to the barn, but the pig is not there. Dad sees the pig on the lawn. The pig is playing with the cat.

Match: The pig was seen on the lawn (Q1)
Mismatch: Dad was seen on the lawn (Q2)

Paul loves to dig for worms. Mom and Dad tell him not to dig in the yard. Paul goes outside to look for worms. Mom sees Paul digging by the fence. Mom tells Sue "Go tell Paul to stop digging near the fence".

Match: Paul was seen near the fence (Q1)
Mismatch: Mom was seen near the fence (Q2)

Mom and Sue are looking for berries. Mom looks for berries along the road. Sue looks in the forest. Mom sees a big bush full of berries. She calls out, "Come here! I found a big bush". Sue hears Mom calling. She comes running towards her.

Match: Mom was heard on the road (Q2)
Mismatch: Sue was heard on the road (Q1)

B. Experiment on constraint on questioning from within a temporal clause

Temporal clause, inanimate question word

1. The rabbit had a nice afternoon.
   First he read the newspaper
   Then he had his supper. He ate hot dogs.
   The rabbit really enjoyed himself.

   What did the rabbit read before eating?
   What did the rabbit eat after reading?

2. The frog got up early. It was a fine morning.
   She sang her favorite pop song.
   Then she read a storybook.
   The frog was then busy with her artwork.

   What did the frog sing before reading?
   What did the frog read after singing?

3. The fox ran down to the river.
   He ate an ice cream cone.
   Then he whistled a tune he's heard on the radio.
   The fox felt pretty happy.

   What did the fox eat before whistling?
   What did the fox whistle after eating?

Temporal clause, animate question word

1. The snake was feeling sad.
   She asked the bear: "Shall I kiss the ostrich?"
   The beard didn't say, but the snake decided to go ahead and kiss the ostrich.
   The snake felt happier.

   Who did the snake ask before kissing?
   Who did the snake kiss after asking?

2. The dog was excited.
He ran up to the cow and asked her, "Shall I chase the sheep?"
The cow didn't answer, but the dog chased the sheep anyway.
The dog enjoyed running.

Who did the dog ask before chasing?
Who did the dog chase after asking?

3. The elephant liked to work.
She asked the tiger, "Shall I help the horse carry those boxes?"
The tiger said "yes!", so the elephant helped the horse.
The elephant was tired at the end of it all.

Who did the elephant ask before helping?
Who did the elephant help after asking?

Complement to V, animate question word

1. The giraffe was bored.
He decided to make up a kind of detective game, finding out where the other animals went.
The giraffe asked the goat, "Will you follow the hippopotamus?"
The giraffe thought this game was really clever.

Who did the giraffe want to follow?

2. The cat was in the garden.
She wanted to help with the gardening.
She asked the chicken, "Shall we help the turtle dig the garden?"
The cat loved being outdoors.

Who did the cat ask to help?

3. The zebra was feeling happy.
He just wanted to hug and kiss everyone.
He asked the lion, "Shall we kiss the monkey?"
The zebra was a kind animal.

Who did the zebra ask to kiss?

Appendix 4
Materials—Passive and Binding Theory Experiments

Act-out

Active sentences

Elephant and lion
The elephant licks the lion

Male pig and female gorilla
The pig tickles the gorilla

Bear and lion
The bear pats the lion

Female gorilla and male pig
The gorilla washes the pig

Passive sentences

Bear and elephant
The bear is washed by the elephant

Male gorilla and female pig
The gorilla is licked by the pig

Lion and bear
The lion is tickled by the bear

Female pig and male gorilla
The pig is patted by the gorilla

Principle A sentences

Female pig and female gorilla
The pig tickles herself

H. Goodluck, *Complex Syntax in the Language of Persons with Down Syndrome*,
SpringerBriefs in Linguistics,
https://doi.org/10.1007/978-3-030-96440-5

Male gorilla and male pig
The gorilla pats himself

Female gorilla and female pig
The gorilla licks herself

Male pig and male gorilla
The pig washes himself

Principle B sentences

Female pig and female gorilla
The pig licks her

Male gorilla and male pig
The gorilla washes him

Female gorilla and female pig
The gorilla pats her

Male pig and male gorilla
The pig tickles him

Judgement task 1

Principle A sentences

Picture: Tom scratches himself	Question: Is Tom scratching himself?
Picture: Jane washes herself	Question: Is Jane washing herself?
Picture: Grandma tickles herself	Question: Is Grandma tickling herself?
Picture: Grandad pats himself	Question: Is Grandad patting himself?

Picture: Jane tickles herself	Question: Is Grandma tickling herself?
Picture: Tom pats himself	Question: Is Grandad patting herself?
Picture: Grandma washes herself	Question: Is Jane washing herself?
Picture: Grandad scratches himself	Question: Is Tom scratching himself?

Principle B sentences

Picture: Tom washes Grandpa	Question: Is Tom washing him?
Picture: Jane tickles Grandma	Question: Is Jane tickling her?
Picture: Grandpa pats Tom	Question: Is Grandpa patting him?
Picture: Grandma scratches Jane	Question: Is Grandma scratching her?

Picture: Tom pats Grandad	Question: is Grandad patting him?
Picture: Jane scratches Grandma	Question: Is Grandma scratching her?
Picture: Grandpa washes Tom	Question: Is Tom washing him?
Picture: Grandma tickles Jane	Question: Is Jane tickling her?

Judgement task 2

Principle A sentences

Show me Tom scratching himself
Show me Jane tickling herself
Show me Grandma washing herself
Show me Grandad patting himself

Principle B sentences

Show me Tom patting him
Show me Jane scratching her
Show me Grandma tickling her
Show me Grandad washing him

Author Index

H. Goodluck, *Complex Syntax in the Language of Persons with Down Syndrome*, SpringerBriefs in Linguistics,
https://doi.org/10.1007/978-3-030-96440-5

Subject Index

H. Goodluck, *Complex Syntax in the Language of Persons with Down Syndrome*, SpringerBriefs in Linguistics,
https://doi.org/10.1007/978-3-030-96440-5

www.ingramcontent.com/pod-product-compliance
Ingram Content Group UK Ltd.
Pitfield, Milton Keynes, MK11 3LW, UK
UKHW021536260726
13993UKWH00002B/538

* 9 7 8 3 0 3 0 9 6 4 3 9 9 *